A WAKE UP CALL

A WAKE UP CALL
Beyond Concepts & Illusions

Sabina Oberoi & Beverly Chapman

RADHA SOAMI SATSANG BEAS

Published by:
J.C. Sethi, Secretary
Radha Soami Satsang Beas
Dera Baba Jaimal Singh
Punjab 143204, India

First edition 2016

21 20 19 18 17 16   8 7 6 5 4 3 2 1

ISBN 978-81-8466-441-6

Printed in India by: Replika Press Pvt. Ltd.

CONTENTS

PUBLISHER'S NOTE

The reader will note that many points made in the book are substantiated by quotations from the writings of the spiritual masters of Beas. All such statements are presented within quotation marks and can be found in the existing publications of the Radha Soami Satsang Beas. The present master's words, however, are not presented in quotation marks as they have not been recorded or published through any media. This is in keeping with his emphasis that spiritual growth is attained through *living* the spiritual teachings rather than through debating the meaning of words and concepts. Notwithstanding the absence of recorded references, words and phrases in this book that are attributed to the present master have been approved by him.

FIRST WORDS

Truth is simple
We are not

The truth we seek is so simple
It's incomprehensible
... to us

So we cling to comforting concepts
And if those concepts make no sense
We cling all the harder

We build walls from illusions
Houses of Me Mine and My
We shut ourselves up inside them
Become prisoners of our mind

Let's go beyond comforting concepts
Let's wake from these dreams and illusions
Let's experience Truth in all its simplicity

Let's get real

WHAT IS
OUR OBJECTIVE?

Of all the saints
who have visited this world
from time immemorial,
none has come to found
a new religion or a new creed.

They have all brought the same message.
They have all preached the same Truth.
They have all shown the same one path....

Unfortunately...
the teachings become perverted
and overlaid with
the conceptions of lesser minds,
unable to grasp their 'real essence'.

MAHARAJ CHARAN SINGH

1

OUR PRESENT POSITION

Words or action?

A ferryman came upon a man floundering and splashing in the water. Leaning far out from his boat towards the drowning man, he called out, "Take my hand."

"I am suffering!" cried the man, continuing to thrash about in the water. "You have no idea how I suffer!"

"Just grab my hand," said the ferryman.

"Oh," the man moaned as he flailed about, "how I long to be back on dry land."

Leaning further out and stretching out closer to him, the ferryman said, "Just take my hand and hold on. I'll pull you into the boat."

"Why has this happened to me?" the man wailed as he went on thrashing around. "It is so unfair (blub, blub) that I should have fallen (blub, blub) into the water."

If you or I were the one in the boat, stretching out our hand, trying to help the drowning man, wouldn't we be tempted to shout in total exasperation,

"COME ON, MAN – TAKE MY HAND. GET REAL!"

Get real! What does that expression mean to us? In today's world it usually implies: Stop kidding yourself. Get a grip on who you are and your situation. Wake up to your reality.

In spirituality, it means all this and more. It also means waking up to what actually is real at the deepest and ultimate level. It means doing what we need to do to experience that reality. It means living that reality, becoming that reality. It actually means God-realization.

Our situation is not so different from the drowning man in the story. When the master tells us to attend to the meditation practice, he is saying, "Here, take my hand. Hold on to it." In other words: Wake up. Attach yourself to Shabd so you don't drown in the vast ocean of life.

As our master tells us over and over again: The real guru is Shabd; the real disciple is the attention attuned to Shabd.[*]

The Shabd is the hand of the Lord, stretching out to us. We have only to grasp that 'hand' and hold on to it instead of floundering and thrashing about, and we will be drawn into a higher level of consciousness.

Happily for us, the present master has not thrown up his hands in exasperation, saying, "Come on, man. Get real!"

Instead he teaches us.

He asks: What do you want? What is your objective?

---

[*]Please see Publisher's Note on page ix to understand our treatment of words attributed to the present master.

He says: Every action can take you toward your goal, or away from your goal.

Are we heading in the direction our master has shown us?

He appeals to our common sense, asking: If your destination lies to the north, and you spend all day walking south, how can you hope to reach your destination?

He tells us we're like patients who go to the doctor – the disease is diagnosed, medicines are prescribed, but then we don't take the medicines and remain sick. We're like hungry people who read recipes but do not take the trouble to cook the food and eat, so naturally, we remain hungry.

How often have we heard the present master say these things? We hear his satsangs – how fervently he pleads with the sangat to attend wholeheartedly to the daily meditation practice – that is, to grasp the hand he is offering us.

If you give me words I'll give you words If you give me action I'll give you action

Do we not feel ashamed when the master has to plead with us? Our living, loving master is all mercy and kindness. How far do we take our heedlessness that he has to resort to scolding us in satsang? How dumb, and foolish, and childish, and self-obsessed are we? What does that say of us as disciples?

However, Sant Mat is not a path of wallowing in feelings of shame and guilt. It is a path of action. It is not a path of flowery words about love. It is a path of action. It is not a path of theories and concepts about the divine. It is a path of action.

As the present master has often said: If you give me words, I'll give you words. If you give me action, I'll give you action.

The choice is ours.

Why did we ask for initiation?

The present master often asks us to think deeply on this. He says: Why did you ask for initiation? There must have been some purpose in it.

Why did we come to Sant Mat? He points out that each one of us has come from some religious or cultural tradition. We are likely to have been members of some community with its own accepted observances, rituals and ways of thinking about life. If we have asked for initiation it must have been because some need of ours was not being met.

What was that need?

He asks us: Did we leave one set of traditions only to latch on to another? Did we ask for initiation merely to join another community whose social conventions and values would give order to our lives? Or did we come to Sant Mat for something more?

Spirituality is not the legacy of any one religion. Spirituality belongs to all religions. The masters have always stressed that practising the spiritual path should make us a better Christian, a better Muslim, a better Hindu, a better Sikh.

We can be a member of any religious community, living up to the highest ideals of that religion, and also dedicate our lives to the mystical path. Equally we can be seekers of Truth and have no religious affiliation, yet dedicate our lives to spiritual practice.

Sant Mat is a spiritual path and has no need to lean on the crutches of blind faith. Nor does it need the crutch of the social observances and celebrations that give form and shape to society. Nor does it need to be propped up on a structure of superstitions or rituals.

The present master has said: The role of the mystic is to help you realize Truth, not to lead you from one illusion to another.

Sant Mat stands on its own – a spiritual path, pure and simple, to be walked by each initiate individually.

You have a living master

In the writings of the saints, great emphasis is placed on the living master, the guru of one's time. The living master is the teacher of the present moment, of the now, who can lead others to Truth.

Why do the saints place such emphasis on the guru of one's own time? Because the outside world, the world of time and space, is always changing. Did it ever change faster than in our present times? A living master not only sees that truth which is eternal, he also sees the specific needs of disciples as per the present moment. He understands our strengths and our weaknesses better than we understand them ourselves.

You might say people catch the spiritual sicknesses of their times. For instance, today we don't like the idea of obedience: we live in a time of the individual – of me, mine, and my life, on my terms, of living how I want to live. We don't like to be told what to do. We also want results quickly. We want them now. We don't want to work hard. The living master knows how to cure the sicknesses of the time. And he gives us a prescription.

As times change, and the forces that influence us change, the saints keep reshaping how they express their timeless teachings. Soami Ji Maharaj says: "Accept the master of the times, I say to you, for your own good." *Vakt guru ko maan tere bhale kee kahoon.*

2

HOW FAR CAN WORDS TAKE US?

Prisoners of words

Mystics speak of a reality that is all oneness. They tell us of a reality that is eternal and unchanging. Yet we who have only experienced a reality that is always changing, where every single thing is temporary and separate, are not equipped to understand oneness. Our mental apparatus of words, symbols and concepts is just not geared to this purpose. That is why it is said that spirituality is not taught, but caught. It is caught from a person who has it, and experienced by the one yearning for it.

When it comes to the spiritual reality, whatever is beyond our own experience is just that: beyond our experience. It is beyond our knowledge, beyond our understanding. It might be someone else's experience; it might be the experience of all the saints in history; but for us it is just a concept.

Every single thing we think we know about the spiritual path that is beyond our own experience is just a concept.

Nothing more. Do we read that there are five spiritual regions? It's a concept. Do we read that our *sinchit** karmas are held in store in the causal plane, and that they will eventually be obliterated through our meditation? It's a concept. Do we read that the Radiant Form of the master awaits us at the eye centre? It's a concept. The only thing we can count on as bedrock reality is what we know through our own experience.

Ideas . . . thoughts . . . concepts . . . metaphors . . . images . . . blah, blah, blah! The problem is that the words of the mystics are so beautiful, so inspiring, so uplifting, we can easily spend our lives studying those words with rapt attention. We can easily *think* we understand. But either we know the truth of those words for ourselves, or we don't.

Our concepts about spirituality give us a sense that we know what's what. We have concepts. We have words. We have ideas, opinions, beliefs. Concepts can orient us in the right direction. But those very concepts can also stand between spiritual experience and us.

Here, then, is our fundamental conundrum: at our current level of consciousness, concepts are the way we form an understanding of anything. We can't help it. That's the way we're made. Yet, by its very nature, the reality we seek is beyond words and cannot be understood through concepts.

What's the solution?

The masters are infinitely practical. They speak to us in our own language, and they point us toward reality. While

---

*Unfamiliar terms are explained in the Glossary at the end of this book.

using words as indicators and pointers, they urge us to take specific action!

Myths and metaphors

To direct our attention to something beyond our current level of understanding, the masters use stories and myths. They use metaphors, analogies and images. They tell us, for example, that if the Lord is like an ocean, then the master is like a wave of the ocean and our soul is like a drop of the ocean.

Once the master used this analogy in a question and answer session and the questioner hesitated, then said, "So . . . we're all going to become water?" This is a perfect example of how the limited parameters of our thinking automatically restrict the master's teachings to the concrete, physical plane of existence that we know. We all do this, in one way or another.

An analogy is not a fact. We are not water, and the purpose of the spiritual path is not for us to become water. The analogy is only a way to point us in the direction of Truth, to orient us. It gives us an idea of the relationship between the master, God, and our soul. But it is not the whole truth about the master, God, or our soul. It is a concept.

Great Master wrote, "Although the Lord, like electricity, pervades everywhere, the master is the point where he shines out as light."

This too is an analogy, an image. It is not the whole truth about the master, but it does give us an idea about why we are so drawn to him. It tells us something about whose light it is that makes the master so attractive to us.

In the Bhagavad Gita we read the story of Arjuna when he asked his beloved master, Lord Krishna, "You say great things. You argue well. But still doubts persist within me because I have not experienced what you talk about. Why don't you give me some experience so my doubts can disappear?"

Lord Krishna replied that he would do so, and then in a flash Krishna became huge; the myriad worlds started rotating around him. It was terrifying and Arjuna thought he was going mad. In great fear he cried out, "Please come back, please come back to your ordinary form. I am frightened."

Lord Krishna resumed his ordinary, human form and said, "I knew you were not ready."

> Spiritual reality can be known only when our consciousness is capable of perceiving it

This, too, is a story. It shows us that the faculties we have available to us limit what we are capable of understanding. It gives us some idea about the nature of the master, but it can't convey the reality. It gives us a concept.

Spiritual reality we can only know once our consciousness has the capacity to perceive it. However, we hear the teachings of the saints and we piece together our own understanding based on our level of consciousness.

Paradoxes

With words a master may plant the seed of awareness, but to understand his meaning we have to go to a higher level of consciousness. For example, the present master often says that meditation is letting go, especially letting go of yourself. Then he also says that meditation is tuning into yourself. How can both of these be true? It's a paradox.

The master will often toss off a one-liner that completely scrambles our thinking. Puzzle over it all we can and we are still left with a mystery.

The present master has been known to say: Burn the books! Yet anyone can see that more and more books are being printed every year by the organization under his direction.

We can't fail to notice that he is building a large library that is intended to become a world-class research library for religion, mysticism, philosophy and spirituality. However, once when a Dera library sevadar asked the master about the purpose of the library, he joked: Maybe I'll have a big bonfire.

What are we to understand of these seemingly paradoxical behaviours and contradictory words? Do we hear his words and get lost in a debate about what he meant? Or do we trust our master and set about doing his real work so we can get to a higher level of consciousness and understand what he's saying to us?

Then again, what does the present master mean when he says, as he often does: Everything is parshad? Parshad, we can easily understand, is a gift from the master to the disciple. But then he says that everything is parshad, and we are baffled. What then is parshad, we ask?

He tells us that everything blessed is parshad. Since the Lord pervades every particle of the creation, isn't every single thing we see, everything we touch, everything all around us blessed? Isn't every breath we breathe a gift from the Lord? Can't we see that our every breath is parshad?

But then, we wonder, why does the master bless those bags of sweets and distribute them to the sangat as parshad? How do these two go together?

The master has a smile on his lips and a twinkle in his eye as he repeats: Everything is parshad.

Master says everything is parshad and we don't understand his words. We only see the gesture, enjoy the beauty of his smile, and forget the words. We cling to the superficiality because we are accustomed to material rewards and cannot break free from these shackles. He gives us a packet of parshad to satisfy our need for outward expression of his love. He continues giving to inspire and motivate us.

The master in his usual mysterious way gives us food for thought and plants the seed of awareness.

What then is parshad? The parshad we receive on the outside is but a minute, small sample of what awaits us inside. He is enticing us, giving us the bait, luring us to take the ultimate gift where everything is parshad. He wants us to look beyond the physical; he wants us to look deep within. He says, if the outside parshad gives us so much happiness, come and receive the parshad inside, experience the gift of inner bliss. Once there, everything is parshad – the good, the bad, the ugly, all, nothing, everything – everything is bliss inside; therefore, everything is parshad.

He is urging us to go inside and realize that the material gifts are not comparable to the bliss experienced inside. There will be nothing to know then because we will be all-knowing; there will be nothing to ask for, because there will be nothing left to gain; there will be no desire, because nothing will be desirable or undesirable. So he says: Look inside, look beyond, look where everything is parshad.

Concepts

If words are unable to convey spiritual reality, why then do the masters use them? Why not just tell us to meditate and then sit in silence, saying nothing about *why* to meditate, nothing about God or the creation, nothing about karma or the pain of separation, nothing about the 'journey' to our 'home'? In fact, why don't they just take us up?

———

There was once a spiritual teacher who would often repeat at the end of his discourse, "Remove the ego self, and realize the truth." Finally, a disciple felt compelled to ask him, "Master, if this is what is needed, why don't you remove the ego self for us and just give us pure truth?"

The master smiled and asked the disciple to get him water to drink. The disciple brought a glass of water and placed it in front of the master.

"What's this?" asked the master.
"This is the water you asked for," answered the disciple.
"But did I ask for a glass or for water?"
The disciple was confused.

"Never mind," the master explained. "Just as you cannot bring water without a vessel, so too, the master cannot express Truth except through concepts."

Trying to convey spiritual teachings without concepts is like trying to bring water without a glass. It is impossible. Water needs a container – it cannot contain itself. In the same way, concepts are the container used by masters of spiritual knowledge to express their teachings.

Concepts have their place. They are an important starting point. They are the kindergarten of the school of spirit. We need the concepts of the saints' teachings to orient us to what is real. Concepts, however, are not the reality.

Concepts are not the reality

The glass holding the water may be expedient; it may even be necessary. But what we're after is the water, not the glass. After all, the same water could be carried in a porcelain teacup, a crystal goblet, or even a plastic water bottle, and still be the same water. What we need to do is to imbibe the essence of the teachings. We need to drink the water.

If we 'drink the water' – that is, if we put the teachings into practice, giving our very best efforts to meditation and the lifelong and unremitting task of training the mind and tuning it to the Shabd – we will go beyond the level of concepts.

Someday we may look back and recognize that the words and concepts which our master used were utterly inadequate to express the reality he was pointing us to. The concepts the masters express are useful when we are spiritual infants, but we want to see beyond them. We look forward to the day when, through our own experience, we will see that the concepts used by the Buddha or Christ or Guru Nanak or any other saints in human history all point to that same one reality – a reality which can only be known through personal experience. But for that we have to do the practice.

Do we really want to stay spiritual infants? Unfortunately, for most of us, we'd rather worship and admire the glass instead of drinking the water. We're quite comfortable enjoying satsang discourses and discussing the lofty principles the masters teach. But when it comes to getting down to the hard, inner work of disciplining and controlling our own minds through the practice of simran – well, we decide we're helpless.

Or we may slip a few of our own ideas into the 'glass of water' the master has poured for us. We adjust the master's teachings and add a few of our own *misconceptions*, creating illusions that we then live in. Our misconceptions appeal to us; they seem reasonable to us, and so when the living master corrects us, we override his teaching with our own 'better understanding'.

What are we doing? As per the story of the master and the glass of water, we are mixing mud into the water and damaging its life-giving properties.

Mud can have many flavours

To make a catalogue of all the ways we – the master's sangat – misconstrue the teachings would fill volumes. But boil it all down and what have we got? One central problem: we try to shape Sant Mat to fit our way of thinking rather than trying to shape our way of thinking to Sant Mat.

Let's face it: our way of thinking is shaped and limited, to an extent far greater than we realize, by our personal backgrounds.

We might come from a particular religion, the religion of our parents and grandparents, and our experience of that religion has shaped our habits, our way of life, and our way of thinking about spiritual reality.

We may have received a particular type of schooling, and our education has shaped our thinking.

Without realizing it, we bring ideas and expectations – along with practices and social conventions – from our own cultural, educational and religious traditions. Since we come from many different backgrounds, we misinterpret the masters' pure teachings in many different ways. Using the metaphor that the teachings are like a glass of pure water, you could say we mix in many kinds of mud, and they all flavour the water differently.

Yet the masters teach that the Truth we seek is one, and cannot be explained by any theory, philosophy or dogma, nor can it be found in any set of traditions or written scriptures. It can never be realized through any rituals or ceremony. Nor can it be found through any superstitious practice. We will realize this when our consciousness is transformed and we merge into Shabd – into Truth itself. For this, we have to follow their instructions.

3

THE CHOICE IS OURS

An 'expiry date' on concepts

The mind is tricky. We hear the master's teachings and we are inspired. But after a period of time, we gradually begin to interpret the teachings to justify our weaknesses. In Maharaj Charan Singh's words, the pure teachings of the saints "become perverted and overlaid with the conceptions of lesser minds, unable to grasp their 'real essence.'"

Isn't that us: the 'lesser minds'? Do we not pervert and overlay the saints' teachings with our own conceptions, our *mis*-conceptions?

The problem is that our conceptions are partial, fragmentary. We understand the world from the limited perspective of our own ego-centred point of view. If three blindfolded people are asked to feel an elephant and describe what it is, one will touch the trunk and say the elephant is a garden hose; one will touch the leg and say it is a tree trunk; one will touch the tail and say the elephant is a rope. Each is in touch with only part of the elephant.

The teachings of the saints come from the vantage point of one who sees the whole, from one who is objective in the most profound sense. But we are like the blindfolded people who are in touch with only part of the whole. We each understand things differently, based on our background and experiences. We even insist that the partial truth we understand is the whole truth, like the blindfolded person clinging to the elephant's trunk and arguing that an elephant is most definitely a garden hose.

The real problem comes, however, when we begin to use our limited understanding of the master's teachings to justify our weaknesses. The master uses words, images and metaphors to convey his teachings to us, but our minds are so tricky we gradually interpret his words in ways that stop our own spiritual development. Once we begin to twist the master's teachings into these harmful misconceptions or illusions, the living master may begin to express the teachings in a different manner to spur us into action. His objective is for us to do the spiritual practice he has taught us, to develop spiritual objectivity ourselves.

To make another analogy: picture a teacher looking up at a cloud in the sky with his students. Let's say the teacher points out how the shape is like a warrior with bow outstretched, poised to shoot. The students understand that the teacher is giving them an ideal and asking them to focus on the warrior's virtues of discipline and fearlessness. Then, after some time the students begin saying, "Well, a warrior is very aggressive, so we too can let our anger explode into violence."

Now the teacher may adjust and point out how the cloud looks like a sailboat, its sails billowing in the wind. And the students understand they should sail gracefully through life letting the wind of the Lord's will blow them where it will, instead of arguing and getting angry over how things work out. But after a while the students begin to say there's no need to put in effort because the Lord's grace does everything.

Now it's time for the teacher to point out that, actually, the cloud looks like a bullock straining with all its might to pull the plough. And that's fine until the students start to . . .

This analogy may sound absurd. However, the living master can discern when a concept is no longer serving a useful purpose – when it has reached its 'expiry date'. Then the living master, with his deep insight into the needs of his living disciples, starts using different words, images and concepts, just as easily as one could change from saying the cloud is like a warrior to saying it is like a sailboat or a bullock.

As soon as we start to think of any concept as the absolute, correct, and only explanation of reality, we are on our way to dogma. In fact, we are well on our way to the intolerance and hatred that characterize all forms of fundamentalism.

Maharaj Charan Singh used to say that we 'arrest' the saints' teachings. 'Arresting' the teachings – an intriguing expression! The saints' teachings are something alive and fluid, something unbounded and infinitely free. Arresting the teachings imprisons them; it traps them in lifeless structures of mental concepts.

What is this need in us to nail down the teachings about spirituality, to fix them firmly in place, secure in a world of concepts? Is it fear? The spiritual reality the saints speak of is so unimaginable, so inconceivable to our minds; it is the ultimate unknown. Fear of the unknown is said to be the root of all fears. Developing concepts about Truth might be our way of holding reality at arm's length, saving us from having to face an unknown reality head-on.

Fear of the unknown, fear of death, of life, of acceptance, of rejection, of illness, of poverty, indeed fear of fear itself – we are slaves of fear. Do we comfort our fearful selves by building our personal shelters from concepts and then inviting Truth to live with us in those small, temporary homes?

Let's just remind ourselves: when we went to the master and asked for initiation onto the path of Shabd, we asked him to show us his world. Through initiation, we committed ourselves to a journey into the unknown. We committed to step out of our self-made prisons, to learn from our master and find out what our master knows. Isn't this why we came to the path?

Truth is simple – we are not

The master's teachings are simple. So extraordinarily simple we just can't get it.

When something is simple, we find it hard to accept. The mind goes into overdrive wondering, why? How can it be so simple? There must be a catch here; there is a trick we've missed. Our minds have such a knack for making simple things complicated.

If something is complicated, the mind just revels in the complexity. If only the master's teachings were more complicated, our hungry minds would have so much more to chew on.

But give the mind a simple solution like two and a half hours of meditation, and we're at a total loss. Because how can it possibly be that simple? There has to be more, something we haven't been told! We might be more satisfied if we were told to stand on our head for three hours, or walk on red-hot coals, or memorize a thousand-page scripture. Now *that* would satisfy our mind. It would even provide a delightful excuse to justify not being able to do it.

The final acid test of whether we correctly understand the masters' teachings is whether we are doing our level best in meditation, whether we are giving full time to the practice daily as instructed at the time of initiation.

On the other hand, even if our understanding of the teachings is riddled with misconceptions – guess what! The practice of meditation will straighten us out. That's why the master keeps telling us to meditate.

An individual choice

As the sangat has grown, now numbering in the millions, the organizational structure necessary to meet the basic needs of the sangat has had to become larger and more complex. Similarly, more and more facilities and buildings are needed at the centres where the sangat meets for satsang. Property, we know from human history, inevitably brings issues of money and power in its wake.

For many of us, the idea of Sant Mat becoming a social rather than spiritual organization is terrifying. It is a nightmare image: a future where all that we have depended upon for spiritual sustenance has gone lifeless. Why this fear?

Seeing the growth of the sangat, we ask ourselves whether the weight of bureaucracy and real estate will bury the spiritual core of Sant Mat under a layer of hierarchy and social conventions.

However, we may take heart.

If we think deeply on it, we will realize that the choice of Sant Mat remaining a purely spiritual path is a decision we each make individually. Sant Mat is a path that is travelled within oneself.

If we get initiated, attend satsang, do seva, but do not attend to meditation, we are essentially acting as members of a social organization.

However, if we attend to meditation daily, keep the vows taken at the time of initiation, and follow the guidance of the living master implicitly, we are following the universal spiritual path. If we are following the master's instructions, we are on a mystical path. Regardless of what others do, we are on the spiritual path of Sant Mat.

The power to turn Sant Mat into merely a social organization is not in the hands of the organization. It is not even a decision made – consciously or unconsciously – by the collective action of the sangat. It is a choice we each make every day when we decide whether or not we will sit down, give the time, and meditate as instructed at our initiation.

The question is not 'out there' but very much 'in here'. It is our decision, a decision for each one of us.

Sant Mat, the practice of Truth, itself cannot be anything other than what it is. 'Sant Mat' signifies the path of the saints. It is an inner path, a way of life demonstrated by the enlightened, which has in its essence remained unchanged since time immemorial, even as the saints' universal teachings have been expressed in different ways according to the changing needs of human beings in different times and different parts of the world.

In Christ's words:
The water that I will give him
shall be in him a well of water
springing up to everlasting life

WORDS,
CONCEPTS & ILLUSIONS

We try to shape Sant Mat
to fit our way of thinking,
rather than trying
to shape our way of thinking
to Sant Mat.

We build walls from illusions

Houses of Me Mine and My

We shut ourselves up inside them

Become prisoners of our mind

We live with these illusions...

4

ABOUT SPIRITUALITY

Once the present master defined 'spirituality' as the awareness of the presence of the divine in every moment of our
everyday lives. Growing in spirituality is growing in awareness. We say that spirituality is the purpose of our lives, but
we have many illusions about what it is and how we might
awaken our latent spirituality. For example:

ILLUSION: Physical objects have spiritual power

In his satsangs, the present master urges the sangat to break
free from the prison of superstitions. To illustrate this point he
often comments that if he were to put a pair of Hazur's (Maharaj
Charan Singh's) shoes in front of the sangat, there would hardly
be a person who would not rush to bow down to them. What,
he asks, have we understood of the masters' teachings?

When he became the master, one of the first things the
present master did was to burn the personal belongings of
the previous masters. Why? He had received many sugges-
tions that these items should be put on display for the sangat.
It was even suggested that he should create a museum to

preserve them for the enjoyment and inspiration of the sangat. Burning these items may have been an extreme measure, but how else could he show that the spiritual path is not about worshipping sacred relics?

Why is it that we tend to associate spirituality with physical things? Why do we imagine that anything physical can be the secret to our own awakening? The well opposite Great Master's house was built with the sole aim of providing water for the sangat, and so it did for fifty years until it had to be closed off. Why? Some of the sangat had begun calling it a well of divine nectar. They were carrying bottles of water home to heal people of sickness, or even to convert them. Some people started to sell the water for personal gain. To put an end to these superstitious activities, the master had to make the water of a perfectly useful well inaccessible.

Similarly, access to the satsang ghar at Dera had to be limited because some members of the sangat began saying the building had a secret, esoteric significance. They began paying homage to the building – bowing down to it, gazing with loving devotion at its spires, speaking of it with awe and reverence. Rumours flew, spreading erroneous ideas such as that it was a replica of a building that exists on some higher plane, or that each turret had some esoteric meaning. Some began calling the building 'Sach Khand' (literally, the realm of truth), confusing it with our spiritual goal, that inner formless truth we seek.

Our real goal is not that easy to reach. Wouldn't it be colossally disappointing if merely visiting a building were all that a life devoted to the highest truth had to offer? Underlining the danger of such an illusion, the present master has said that if we continue bowing to the satsang ghar, he will not hesitate to tear the building down.

Sant Mat is not a path of idol worship; it's not a path of revering physical objects. On a spiritual path, devotion to a building, a statue, a photograph, or any other form of inert matter is a dead end, because that which is dead and unconscious cannot lead to spiritual life and awakened spiritual consciousness.

Throughout human history, holy shrines have been created so people could benefit from the peace and quietness of these places to remember the Lord and to practise their devotion. But what happens when we start considering them as holy buildings? Instead of praying inside them, we start praying *to* them.

Unfortunately, many of us associate the path of spirituality with superstition, engaging in activities that we believe can bring about supernatural results. One of the young people in a question and answer session in the *pandal* (the satsang venue) at Dera said his mother and grandmother told him that every step he took going to the Dera erased karmas. What was the master to say to such a notion? He patiently explained that these kinds of superstitions have nothing to do with eliminating our karmic load.

There is a difference between superstitious action and action rooted in deep and matured devotion. Consider the story of Queen Draupadi related in the Mahabharata. Lord Krishna told the royal family that their penance would be accepted in heaven only if Supach, a holy man of low and humble birth, attended their feast, and if the divine bell sound was heard from the sky. When Supach said he would not attend unless he was given the merits of 101 Ashvamedh Yagyas,* everyone despaired, since no one had accomplished even one single Ashvamedh Yagya and they could hardly give him merits they did not have.

As the story goes, Queen Draupadi herself prepared several delicious dishes and walked barefoot all the way to Supach's hermitage. She told him that she had heard that if a person with love and devotion in their heart walks to see a saint, every step taken has the merit of an Ashvamedh Yagya, and therefore she could give him 101 of those merits. Supach now accepted the food. Before eating it, however, he shocked Queen Draupadi by mixing all the dishes together as if he had no idea that each one was a delicacy to be savoured. Appalled, Queen Draupadi thought to herself that Supach really must be a person of no education and no refined taste.

Supach finished eating, yet the divine bell sound did not ring. No one knew what to do. Lord Krishna explained that the problem lay in the mind and thoughts of Queen Draupadi. When the queen realized her mistake, she humbled her mind and prayed in her heart for forgiveness for her arrogant and wrong thinking. At that moment, the bell sound was heard.

We read these stories in the scriptures and miss the point. In this case we latch on to the idea that each step taken to see a saint accrues merits in heaven. However, as the story illustrates, it was not the steps taken, but rather the humbling of Draupadi's mind which made the divine bell sound ring

---

*Ashvamedh Yagya is a sacred Vedic sacrificial rite that can only be conducted by a king.

out. Focusing on merits for each step taken is superstition, not devotion.

Some of us even use parshad superstitiously. We send parshad to the sick, believing it will cure them. We feed parshad to children, believing its magic powers will make them decide to follow the spiritual path. What will we see next? Little shops selling parshad as holy trinkets?

The masters have repeatedly explained that parshad is not a magic pill. It has no healing powers. And it is not in our hands to pull anyone to the path, not even our own children. The pull to follow the spiritual path is purely individual. It comes from within, from the Lord. But rather than accepting parshad as a personal gift from our beloved friend, our master, we'd rather use it as a magic talisman!

> **A sure way to arrest the teachings is to send reasoning and common sense out the window**

ILLUSION: Spirituality demands blind faith

Some of us insist that once we have accepted the teachings of the masters, our faith should be firm and unshakeable. To question or have doubts, we say, is unacceptable! Shocking! Disrespectful! Having faith, we think, means fervently hanging on to a belief through thick and thin. If we are taught a concept and we continue to believe it without any evidence to confirm it, we call it 'faith'.

The present master takes the opposite approach. He says: Don't have blind faith. Ask questions. In question and answer sessions he often encourages the confused questioner, saying: Reason with me. Once he said: A sure way to arrest the teachings is to send rationality, reasoning and common sense out the window.

In countless satsangs the present master has even challenged the audience, asking: How do you know I'm not a fraud?

How *do* we know? We will have to develop a higher level of consciousness before we will know who or what the master is. Meanwhile, the master encourages us to ask questions. In fact, he says, we should continue to ask questions as long as we have questions.

Why is he encouraging us to question when we know that ultimately faith, obedience and surrender are key to the life of a disciple? The fact is, if we suppress our questions due to the false notion that we must start with blind faith, we may well remain with rigid beliefs that do not lead to spiritual experience. Yet in the sphere of spirituality there are many questions that are not resolved, despite our longing, because they can't be resolved at our level of consciousness. Rather, at some point they just fade out. We become satisfied just to know that we have a method to reach that higher consciousness. So, we figure, we might as well get on with our spiritual practice.

Do we need some sort of faith just to get started? Sure. But it is not the type of faith built on holding a tight grip on some belief that we have no way of knowing for ourselves. It's more like the 'faith' a scientist needs in order to start an experiment and stick with it to its completion. The scientist doesn't know whether his hypothesis is accurate or not, but somehow he is still able to put long hours and arduous, painstaking effort into the experiment. Why? Because he's pretty sure the method of the experiment is correct and it will effectively prove or disprove the hypothesis.

And so, with the spiritual path, we just need to get started on a life of practice. The practice itself will unveil that truth we can't know now. All in good time, with practice.

If we insist on blind faith from the start we can stunt our own spiritual growth. If we insist that others should exhibit unquestioning blind faith – for example, if we pressure young-sters to adhere to the faith, or if we judge, shun or ostracize those who raise questions – we are treating the sangat not as seekers of Truth, but as believers claiming they know Truth and protecting their claim in a fortress of dogma.

ILLUSION: Spirituality means morality so who needs meditation?

Spirituality can only grow and thrive in a nurturing soil of morality. To pursue spiritual awakening without having a moral foundation to one's life is like planting a crop in soil drenched in poisonous herbicidal chemicals. The green leaves unfurl vibrant with life, only to turn black, shrivel and fall off.

However, the spiritual path requires more than moral val-ues. It requires training the mind to focus, to contemplate and to listen to the Shabd. While morality is essential for manag-ing our lives in the physical world, the spiritual path is about raising our consciousness to a higher level to experience the reality that lies beyond the physical and mental realms.

Recently the present master gave a series of satsangs on dharma. Many of us, of course, were confident we knew what dharma was. Dharma, as anyone can tell you, means duty and responsibility, particularly moral or religious responsibility. We generally think of dharma as religion, or as the codes of conduct that govern our lives, the rules and norms that keep society in balance and functioning well.

The master explained eloquently that the real dharma of a human being is unique. Our true dharma, our highest responsibility as human beings, is self-realization and God-realization. Attending to the meditation practice as instructed by a true saint is fulfilling the true dharma of a human being.

If we ignore that true dharma, the unique dharma of being human, we are missing the essence of the spiritual path and the essence of our humanity.

There is always the tendency to focus on the outward, visible, measurable aspects of life – to assess and pass judgement. Who knows whether anyone else is, or is not, attending daily to meditation? It's a private matter and no one else can know or judge our sincerity. But we do so like to judge one another! In any group of people, how quick we are to view the community as a place to enforce a kind of 'group morality'. If we concern ourselves with the moral rules of conduct and leave aside the spiritual pursuit that is our unique dharma, then we are laying the groundwork for a social and moral institution and nothing more.

Our highest responsibility as human beings is self-realization and God-realization

ILLUSION: Spirituality can be measured by appearances

It would seem we human beings are naturally prone to making judgements, even on the most superficial basis. Within the sangat we sometimes create artificial distinctions that have no validity on a spiritual path. For example, sometimes Westerners imagine that the Indian sangat is more spiritual than they are. They see Indian initiates as more devotional, more humble. When asked, the master consistently says that each disciple struggles with the same challenges: training and conquering the mind. It's the same all over.

Some initiates who come from a Sikh background may think that only Sikhs can properly understand the teachings of Shabd. After all, aren't most of the satsangs delivered at Dera based on writings from the Adi Granth? On the other hand, some initiates from other countries think they have a better handle on understanding the master's teachings than people from India. Their understanding, they believe, is more objective. They believe they can see past the traditional language and symbols that come from Indian culture.

And so it goes. Divisions and prejudices: Are women more spiritual or are men more spiritual? Are the Chinese initiates more disciplined? Are the African initiates more devotional?

These cultural generalizations are meaningless. We each have to use our own strengths to overcome our weaknesses. We each are on a journey into the interior of our own human reality to self-realization, then God-realization. What we have in common is so much greater than any cultural distinctions that separate us. We are all children of the same one power and divine energy, all seeking to return to our source, our shared true home.

We need to see each other simply as human beings. We need to embrace our common heritage as fellow seekers and fellow human beings on a journey to Truth.

ILLUSION: A spiritual path should meet our social needs

The present master has said that socializing and social events are one of the fastest ways to lose the spiritual essence of the saints' teachings.

Naturally, we are social creatures and we have social needs. Religions throughout the world attempt to answer both the spiritual needs and the social needs of their practitioners. They fulfil a much-needed social function through annual, monthly or weekly gatherings, ranging from festivities and feasts to solemn occasions marking the passage of major life events.

The present master has said: It is rare to find a spiritual path which focuses solely on spirituality.

The master intends to lead us on that rare path.

As the sangat has grown and satsang centres have been built in various cities around the world, there is growing pressure from many of us to use satsang centres to fulfil social, family or community needs. The present master has been absolutely clear that satsang centres have two purposes, and two purposes only: satsang and seva. Both of these are spiritual pursuits intended to help us in our main spiritual pursuit – meditation.

Notwithstanding his guidance, we ask why there can't be social gatherings at the centres, or even celebrations like Christmas or Diwali parties. We ask why there can't be soccer games or activities for children while the parents do seva so that the whole family can enjoy a day at the centre. We seem eager to turn the satsang centres into community and social centres, taking the place of gurdwaras, temples and churches in fulfilling certain family and community needs.

The master gives us unfailing guidance to save us from losing the focus of the spiritual path by mixing it with social and community needs. He is steadfast and unwavering in his wish to turn our attention within. He gives his instructions for the spiritual benefit of the living sangat. He reminds us that ours is an inward journey.

5

ABOUT INITIATION

At the time of initiation we are given the instructions on how to meditate, along with guidelines for living a Sant Mat way of life. At initiation we make a commitment, taking solemn vows to be vegetarian; avoid mind-altering and addictive substances, namely alcohol, drugs and tobacco; lead a clean, moral life; and spend two and a half hours a day in the meditation practice – every day for the rest of our lives.

Does something esoteric also happen at initiation?

We may read that at initiation we are connected to the Shabd, but we may also read that the Shabd is already within us and has always been there, sustaining us, moment by moment. We may read that the master places his Radiant Form within us, but we may also read that the master is Shabd and that Shabd is formless.

We may read that the master takes over the administration of our karmas. Yet we also read that the master does not interfere with or change our fate karmas – the events and situations that are allotted for us to go through during this life.

We may read that at the time of creation certain souls didn't want to incarnate and the Lord has now sent his son to collect those very rare few souls. Yet the master also tells us that the Lord loves each and every being, each and every particle of the creation, equally. The Lord has no favourites. If he did, the master says, he would not be worthy of our devotion.

Whatever happens at an esoteric level at the time of initiation is beyond our comprehension. To understand the apparent paradoxes and mysteries we will have to go to a higher, finer level of consciousness.

What we know for sure is that we receive instructions on how to reach that higher, finer level of consciousness, and we make a firm commitment to follow the instructions. The master asks us to focus on the practical side of his instructions rather than speculate on any esoteric aspect of initiation.

Focus on the practical side of the master's initiation instructions

This is one of the principal thrusts of the present master's teaching: he encourages us to get on with the practice of discipleship and not to analyse or worry about or try to understand the path with the intellect. He counsels us not to speculate. Our illusions derive from just such speculation.

ILLUSION: Only four births after initiation

In the writings of Sant Mat we find the statement that once initiated, it takes a maximum of four births to achieve permanent liberation. Unfortunately, today we take this to mean that initiation is a kind of guarantee. It's an insurance policy. By showing up for the ceremony of initiation, we've paid the premium and now it's all taken care of. No need to put any great effort into meditation because the ceremony of initiation has already guaranteed liberation, if not in this lifetime, then within four lifetimes.

Haven't we ever speculated: Hmmm, this must be my first or second life on the path, because I'm still deeply engrossed in worldly pursuits, and there sure isn't enough time for meditation. Clearly, this is not the lifetime in which I will reach liberation. Well anyway, I will be better in the next life, because with that four-life guarantee the master will have to arrange things that way.

Isn't this the way we sometimes think? How easily we absolve ourselves of responsibility.

The master repeats again and again that so long as we are more interested in this world than in spiritual reality, we will not be liberated. So long as our desires are entangled here, we will stay here. What to say of four lives, an infinite number of lives won't change that fact. It's a law of nature. We go where our desires are. Nature takes its course. Until and unless we actually do the meditation, absorb ourselves in simran, turn our attention away from material existence to divine reality, we cannot be liberated from repeated births and deaths.

In the words of Great Master: "Your reference to the maximum of four lives is rather amusing. There is absolutely no compulsion to finish your pilgrimage here in the compass of four lives only. In fact, nobody can go up as long as he has desires on the earth plane. They will surely drag him down. The master can show the way and help you along the path, but does not force you. Please note that it is a privilege and not an obligation."

Wait a minute, you say, doesn't initiation involve some kind of guarantee? Doesn't the master promise that once initiated we will certainly be liberated sooner or later? Hasn't he said that there are no failures in Sant Mat?

Sardar Bahadur Ji made the situation clear when he said that for those who don't attend to their meditation, the master may need to apply the soap of poverty, disease and dishonour. Do we really want to go that way? If we don't take advantage of the opportunity of this life, the next life may need to be very unpleasant to convince us of the need to get down to our spiritual work.

The present master has explained that when any masters of the past said there was a maximum of four lives, they were referring to the four stages of spiritual growth. Soami Ji Maharaj says: "*Ek janam guru bhakti kar janam doosare naam, janam teesare mukti pad chauthe mein nij dhaam.*" "One life devote yourself to the guru; for the second life, to Nam; the third life, then, is the state of liberation; and the fourth, our real home."

How often have we heard the present master say that if we have been initiated we can make this lifetime our last one? We can do it. He tells us that the master would not have initiated us if he didn't believe we could do it. He says that the master has more confidence in us than we have in ourselves. We only have to be obedient to the instructions given at initiation, and he will take care of the rest.

ILLUSION: Our way of life can remain unchanged

Some of us think our way of life can remain essentially unchanged after initiation. We think we can basically keep the vows, but go right on with all the same priorities and same commitments as before. We seem to think that, given the greatness of our master, our lives will be fruitful spiritually without making any sacrifices or major adjustments.

It's like someone who makes a decision to go on a diet and lose ten kilos. Suppose they make a formal, public resolution to do so. Then they go on eating exactly the same amounts they have always eaten, doing no more exercise than they have always been doing, and they think some magical force will cause the kilos to fall off them.

It is this type of magical thinking that trips us up. Some of us even take the third vow very loosely. To live a clean, moral life, we think, is only a very broad, general guideline. Or it only refers to earning an honest living and remaining sexually faithful to your spouse. Does it matter if we cheat in business? Tell a lie? Take something that isn't ours?

But what if everyone we know cheats on their taxes and it is considered normal? Do we think there will be no consequences if we don't pay what's due? What if everyone in our community thinks it is normal for men to abuse or harass their wives? Can we hurt any living being without consequences to our own spiritual development? Can we simply follow customs without inviting their karmic repercussions?

The present master has often repeated: Everything matters; everything we do counts. As he is fond of saying: Every penny makes a pound.

Every action of ours can either take us toward the Lord or away from the Lord. There can be no spirituality where there is no morality. The present master continually reminds us that initiation is not a 'rubber stamp'. At initiation the master does not 'stamp' us with the label 'satsangi'. As Sardar Bahadur Ji said: "One does not become a satsangi simply by being initiated. One must mould his life in accordance with the principles of satsang. Every thought, speech and action must conform to them. Actions speak louder than words."

ILLUSION: No return to the animal kingdom

Do you believe that once initiated you won't be reborn as an animal or plant or anything other than a human being, no matter what? Both Maharaj Sawan Singh and Maharaj Charan Singh have assured disciples of this great benefit of initiation. Yet it is not as black and white as we might assume.

The problem with this concept lies with us and with how we misinterpret the statements of the masters. Today some of us go so far as to claim that no matter what we do – no matter how cruel or greedy or licentious we might be – if we have been initiated we will always get a human birth next time.

Wow! If we were to act on that assumption, what a dangerous trap that would be! If it were true, we'd have *carte blanche* to commit murder, adultery, robbery, and yet somehow be vindicated and unaccountable. In fact, it would imply that once we are initiated, the law of karma ceases to operate.

Do we really think we've been certified with the 'stamp' of initiation and now we are above the law? Do we think that the karmic law applies to everyone else, but not to us? When queried about this so-called guarantee that once initiated we can't and won't take a birth as an animal, the present master responded: Why not?

How disturbing it was to us all to hear his response! We liked the idea that we had a guarantee.

Can there really be a discrepancy between the teachings of the present master and his predecessors? The present master expanded on his response to help us understand it: Yes, an initiate can be reborn in one of the lower species, for if our actions befit an animal, why not? But it is up to the master to decide what is best for each initiate.

Great Master said that if someone "has done the actions of animals and not of man, he will go back to the class of animals." Those chilling words should put aside any arguments on this subject.

Our cherished beliefs, no matter how comforting, cannot alter the fact that our actions will determine the form in which we are reborn. This is the law, and the masters tell us repeatedly that saints do not contravene the law of creation.

While mere thoughts do not generate karmic reactions, each thought we entertain creates a mental impression, which leads to action sooner or later if repeated. It is said:

> Sow a thought and reap a deed,
> Sow a deed and reap a habit,
> Sow a habit and reap a character,
> Sow a character and reap a destiny.

We will be born to the level of our consciousness. No wild delusions can remove the fact that we, each one of us, have to face the karmas we set in motion for ourselves.

So we do well to ask ourselves: Do my actions befit an initiate of a perfect master in their unfailing human kindness, temperance and humility? Does my consciousness reflect this high spiritual potential, or at least a firm uncompromising aspiration to grow in that direction?

At this level of the creation, the law of karma rules supreme, dictating whether we return as a human being to continue to work with this highest of opportunities or whether we are reborn as a pig, a monkey, or in any other form. Whether we are initiated or not, the law remains: as the seed, so the fruit. Whoever causes misery suffers. Whoever causes well-being enjoys happiness. Like for like, action and reaction. The masters do not break nature's laws.

ILLUSION: Hey! We need those guarantees! They help us!

How the present master has shocked the sangat by calling into question the 'guarantees' we thought we had! He explains to us so often that masters look to the nature of the times in which they live and adjust the way they teach to the particular strengths and weaknesses of their sangat. Times change, as do the strengths and weaknesses of the people. It is the master of our times – the living master – who frames the teachings in a way that can help today's disciples use their strengths to overcome their weaknesses.

What are our strengths and weaknesses?

The danger in this present age of limitless material plea-sures, instant gratification and knowledge delivered in easily digested sound bites is that we look for the shortcut, the quick fix, the easy answer.

In today's world, the idea of a guarantee clearly does not serve us well. Oh, how convenient to think that all we really needed to do was to show up at initiation so that the master would have to keep his promise to liberate us, while we, for our part, have no responsibility.

In past eras too, the masters addressed the disciples of their time. Just think how some past masters put their dis-ciples through rigorous tests for years before giving them the gift of initiation. Who today could pass such tests? If past masters 'guaranteed' liberation in four lives and no return to the animal king-dom, we can only guess they understood their own disciples. Maybe they knew that their disciples, overwhelmed with gratitude, would devote their utmost to meditation, without reservations, conditions and limitations.

Initiation is an opportunity not a guarantee

Yet wait a minute, you say: This idea of the *living master* adjusting according to the needs of the times is all very well and good. But what are the facts? Just the cold, hard facts. Is there or isn't there a four-life maximum? Can we or can we not be reborn as an animal?

To truly understand the answer to these questions we will have to go to a higher level of consciousness where we can see the workings of creation for ourselves. Meanwhile, it is more useful to ask: How does it make a difference? These are, for us, only concepts. What we know for sure is that we are alive right now . . . in a human form and initiated. Right now we have an opportunity.

Initiation has powerful purpose and potential. It is an opportunity, not a guarantee.

ILLUSION: Six months of meditation ensures enlightenment

You may have heard that the master assures us we will be enlightened if we meditate for six months. What a dangerous trap that idea is!

If we set a time limit for our enlightenment, we will surely be disappointed. What happens when six months go by and no enlightenment is in sight? Will we blame the path and the master and abandon the practice?

Where did this idea – which is so popular – come from? It may have come from a well-known and oft-repeated anecdote. A woman came to Great Master and begged him to fulfil her wish to have a child. He reasoned with her. He advised her to accept the Lord's will. But she begged again and again and would not relent. Finally he told her first to meditate for six months and then come back and ask again. When she returned after six months she told him she no longer wanted a child. She was so happy in her meditation.

The fact is that we don't know what the woman was experiencing. We only know that her fervent and obsessive desire for a child had evaporated – a craving so fierce that she had gone to the master to beg him to intervene in her karmas and grant her a child. Perhaps her practice of meditation had brought her peace of mind. Perhaps a certain clarity came into her way of thinking and she could now see how the craving for a child upset her equilibrium and made her unnecessarily miserable. Perhaps with six months of meditation practice she could feel relaxed and contented in going through her karmas – karmas which might not include a child.

We like to think she experienced enlightenment, which we probably assume included lots of interesting visions and a dramatic journey into higher realms. Actually, we don't know what enlightenment looks like. What we know for sure is that her attitude changed. That in itself is a sign of spiritual progress. But it is a type of progress we prefer to over-look as unimportant.

This idea that six months of meditation ensures enlighten-ment could also have come from an answer one of the masters gave to a disciple's query, or from a letter a master may have written in answer to a particular initiate. We need to remem-ber that each one of us has a different background, a different karmic load. We have different perspectives on life. We take different approaches to following the master's instructions. So the master's answers are tailored to individual disciples.

How could there be any specified time limit for reaching enlightenment? Does it stand to reason? Is it even common sense to think so? What to say of six months, could we reason-ably say that absolutely every disciple will reach enlighten-ment in a year? Or ten years? Forty years? Could there possibly be any absolute time limit that applied to everyone?

Great Master stated the point categorically: "Sant Mat does not fix any time limit."

In a letter to an initiate, he explained: "No period can be fixed as to when the attention of any person will begin to stay within the focus. It depends upon the longing, faith, perseverance, and his past record." In another letter, he wrote: "Again, there is no fixed time limit in any system, in which time a practitioner will reach the stage [of going within at the eye centre]. If anybody fixes the time limit, he is deceiving himself and deceiving others."

The masters have all stressed the importance of approaching meditation without expectations. Sitting in meditation without any expectations settles us into the right frame of mind for spiritual practice. When we attend to meditation without looking for results, we can be focused. We can be relaxed.

In any case, how can we have expectations when we don't have a clue what to expect? If the spiritual path is a journey, it is a journey into the unknown.

6

ABOUT THE SANGAT

The sangat, the community of initiates of the master, can serve a very positive function in the life of a seeker of spirituality. When we come together for satsang in the company of like-minded seekers, we are reminded of the purpose of our lives. We can each derive encouragement and inspiration to stay firm on the lofty principles of Sant Mat. The sangat can provide opportunities to us for selfless service. In our ego-bound state such service can be a great help in developing humility and the qualities that support spiritual growth.

The present master has referred to the sangat as a 'support group'. There are all sorts of support groups in the world, ranging from those for cancer survivors to those for parents with disabled children. In a support group we learn from others who share the same struggles as we do. We are heartened and encouraged. Barriers come down and we feel less alone. On the path each one of us strives – in silence and solitude – to please the master with our daily spiritual practice. The sangat can help us keep up the courage to remain steadfast.

However, some of our illusions about the sangat can turn this 'support group' into a confusing and possibly negative force in our life. Such as . . .

ILLUSION: Satsangis are special, and non-satsangis are . . .

Many of us label everyone who has been initiated as 'satsangi', and call other people 'non-satsangis'. In this way we view the sangat as if it were an exclusive club, as if all the 'members of this club' are special, or even superior to those who are not initiated. Calling people satsangis or non-satsangis, or even 'Radha Soamis', we slip mindlessly into the age-old human tendency of drawing a sharp line between 'us' and 'them'. Incalculable harm has been done throughout human history by this tendency to divide 'us' from 'them'.

In his satsangs, the present master often hammers home the point that Hazur spent forty years helping us to go beyond our religions, castes, countries and colour. So why, he asks, are we creating new boundaries?

What do we mean when we say, "I come from a satsangi family," or "Do you come from a satsangi family?" How can a family be 'satsangi'? *Sat* means truth, and *sang* means association with. Satsangi means one who is in the company of truth. A real satsangi is one who has merged in the Shabd, merged in spiritual Truth. The rest of us are seeking. We might call ourselves initiates. We might call ourselves seekers. If we're honest and think clearly, we'd hesitate to call ourselves satsangis.

Some of us frame our choice of a marriage partner in terms of satsangi vs. non-satsangi. Some of us name our business Radha Soami Grocery Shop or Baba Ji Taxi Service. We print stickers or paint Radha Soami on our cars to advertise to the world that we belong to the 'satsangi' club.

What are we doing? Aren't we treating our master's sangat as if it were an exclusive social group? Aren't we making a division of us vs. them? When we label others as non-satsangis, do we judge them as being either inferior or somehow misguided or just simply 'not one of us'?

The present master has repeatedly said that we would be very arrogant if we said ours is the only path to God, or that our master is the only master. Arrogance and spirituality pull in opposite directions. If we harness two bullocks to a cart, one on the front end, the other on the back end, and they both start pulling with all their might, the cart will go nowhere.

In question and answer sessions whenever a questioner refers to someone as a non-satsangi, the present master says something like: How does it make a difference? We are all seekers. A satsangi is one who has realized the Shabd. We are still seeking, so there is no difference.

And when anyone complains about others criticizing our way of life, he says something like: If you want them to respect your way of life, you have to respect their way of life. Who are we to say our philosophy is right and theirs is wrong? He often points out that the Lord's love is there for each and every being in equal measure. In the Lord's eyes, all the distinctions we make – caste, creed, religion – do not exist. For the Lord, we are all souls yearning for union with him.

When you look at all the traditional religions in the world, you can easily see that they serve many positive functions for the well-being of humanity. They promote good moral values. They inculcate a devotional and respectful frame of mind. They inspire service to the most deprived members of society. They give people an anchor in life, providing the strength to face the ups and downs of life. They have even inspired great works of art and music and magnificent buildings.

However, most religions do one thing that is clearly the opposite of the mission of the saints and mystics. Religions tend to divide, where mystics unite. Religious communities have boundaries that mark those who belong to them as distinct from those who do not. The religion then becomes a label, so we can say, "I am an X." And "He is a non-X."

Let's not divide God's undivided family into 'us' and 'them'

Someone once brought Baba Farid a pair of scissors. Baba Farid spoke for all mystic saints of all times when he responded: "Don't bring me scissors; bring me a needle and thread. I don't cut apart; I sew together."

Christ said, "Do not think that I came to destroy the Law or the Prophets. I did not come to destroy but to fulfil." What is that Law? It is the law of love. The living master, the guru of the times, is always needed to remind us how to fulfil that one unchanging law because we are so inclined to divide and judge.

Let's face it, it is natural, natural to our highest nature, to be flooded with gratitude for the great gift of initiation. If we feel we've been the recipients of grace far beyond our deserving, we're right. Let's allow this awe and gratitude to spur us on to live the Sant Mat way of life and do our best with the daily meditation practice. Let's not twist the natural feelings of awe and gratitude into arrogance, intolerance and narrow-mindedness.

Let's not turn the sangat into the scissors that cut the family of God's beloved creatures into 'us' and 'them'.

The tendency to divide the human race into 'our community' and 'not our community' has been the source of endless hatred and intolerance. Throughout history it has incited the violence that has inflicted so much pain and suffering on God's creatures. Do we really want to go down that road?

ILLUSION: It's our duty to enforce Sant Mat values in the sangat

The master teaches us that while each one of us must navigate complex moral dilemmas in our lives, doing our best to make the right decisions, it is wrong to think we should judge others or try to enforce spiritual principles. The masters themselves do not judge. They are always loving and positive. As Maharaj Charan Singh often used to point out, if the masters were to expose our weaknesses, who would come to them? The masters, he would say, do not come to condemn us; what more condemnation can there be than that we are separated from the Father?

Each initiate has an individual relationship with the master; each struggling seeker after Truth has an individual relationship with the Lord within. Neither the general sangat nor sevadars in positions of responsibility are there to judge or punish anyone.

Maharaj Charan Singh made this point in particularly strong terms. Countless times he was asked how initiates should respond to others who had strayed from the principles of Sant Mat. He always stressed that we should not even make anyone conscious of their weaknesses. What was important, he said, was that anyone who wished to come to satsang, or to do seva, should feel welcome. As a sangat, inspired by the example of our master, we are there to love, support and serve one another with humility and kindness.

We could each ask ourselves how we got so lucky as to be welcomed into satsang. We could reflect on the words of Soami Ji: "Really, the *jeev* is not entitled to satsang. . . . Only after attending satsang for some time would he become worthy of sitting there." A *jeev* is a living being, an ordinary person. In other words, you and me.

Once, in a monastery, a theft took place and the monks asked the abbot to identify and punish the thief. The abbot took no action. Some days later, again a theft took place, and the monks asked the abbot to send the thief out from the monastery. Again the abbot took no action. The monks then said they would all leave the monastery if action were not taken. The abbot said, "You are all free to leave the monastery, if you like, because you know that thievery is wrong. But how can I ask the thief to leave? Without the tolerance, compassion and clear principles of the monastery, how will he ever learn right from wrong?" Tears streamed down the face of the thief. He never stole again.

> The sangat is there to love and support
> each other with humility and kindness

ILLUSION: The RSSB sangat represents an 'ideal world'

When we learn about the master and the noble teachings he gives us as guidance in how to live a moral and ethical life, many of us imagine that the sangat is made up of exemplary people. We think we have joined a group where everyone is kind, honest and scrupulous in their moral standards.

We then take on business partners assuming they are honest in all their dealings simply because they are initiated. And then we are shocked when we find our partner has cheated us or embezzled money. Or we choose a 'satsangi' marriage partner assuming that the 'satsangi' label means the partner is a good person. Then we are shocked if someone turns out to be bad-tempered and violent, or lazy and dishonest.

With this illusion we have certainly opened ourselves to disappointment, to disillusionment! We have to remember that initiates on the path are just like everyone else. We have to use our common sense in our dealings with each other.

When we start on the path, we start from wherever we are. We are all ordinary human beings, no different from anyone else, certainly no better, hopefully no worse. It has been said that the master does not look around to find the most holy and wonderful people for his initiates. Why we were selected, why the pull to follow the spiritual path was felt by us and not by someone else, we don't know.

Once the present master was asked how or why it happened that some of us were pulled to the path to be initiated by Maharaj Charan Singh. He said with a smile: Maharaj Ji just picked us up from the side of the road.

ILLUSION: Representatives are evolved souls

Some initiates believe that anyone who is appointed a representative must be spiritually elevated. After all, we hear their satsang discourses and feel inspired. Where does that inspiration come from? We may have received the initiation instructions from a representative, standing for the master. So we think the representative must be a denizen of some high spiritual plane. Sometimes we may even say, "I was initiated by so-and-so," naming the representative who gave us the instructions.

When representatives give the instructions they are representing the master and acting on our master's behalf. That's what 'representative' means. They are not initiating anyone. The master of the time initiates us.

The flip side of the coin is just as much an illusion. Some of us don't want to receive initiation through a representative, believing that it is not the same thing as being initiated by the master. We think the representative is just an ordinary person, and therefore attending an initiation in India with the master physically present is different, more valid, more real.

The power to initiate is with the master. The truest thing that can be said about the representatives is this: the representatives are just sevadars. It does not help to pour adulation their way, to transfer to them the outer obeisance that the master does not want. Why put them on a pedestal? The mind seeks hierarchy; it wants outer realities toward which it can direct its attention, its veneration, its observances. Our path, however, is inward and any external focus simply distracts us from what is real.

ILLUSION: The master's close associates must be spiritually elevated

In earlier times when travel was at the speed of a horse or a bullock cart and the fastest means of communication was a hand-carried letter that made its slow way over mountains and across plains, the sangat of any master was relatively small. The distance from where the master resided to the disciple living farthest away was not so great. In some cases time spent in the master's company meant sitting with him along with just one or two others. Or in a gathering of twenty . . . or forty . . . or a hundred or so.

Not so anymore.

In our modern era of high-speed travel and telecommunications, the present master's sangat is huge. Not only does the sangat number in the millions, it is also spread to the farthest corners of the world. Even though the master himself travels around the world to visit his sangat, how many initiates spend time with him one-to-one? Or in a small family-style group? How many see him often, and all through the year? Even when not actually seeing him, how many live and work physically near to his home? The answer to all these questions is only a very small percentage of the sangat.

Naturally, then, some initiates imagine that the master's family members and close associates must be elevated souls. Spending so much time with the master in such a close and personal setting, they must be blessed with a special grace. To take meals with the master, to spend an evening in relaxed conversation, to take a cup of tea together with the master – we can hardly imagine such a blessing. Perhaps we even think the master's family members are to be revered.

Innumerable times the master has said: The sangat is my family. He even says his family and long-time friends, due to proximity and familiarity, are at a disadvantage – and he quotes the well-known words said about Guru Nanak Dev: *Baabe tare chaar chak, baakee rah gae chaar, sahure, peke, naanke, aur langotiya yaar.* The meaning is that Guru Nanak travelled in all the four directions and many people became disciples from far and wide, but four groups of people 'languished ashore and missed the boat' – his in-laws, his father's family, his mother's family and his childhood friends.

We need to look to the master's presence within us

As disciples, we are the master's real family. He is the spiritual master through and through, and he is responsible for reuniting our soul with its source. There cannot be a closer bond than the bond between a true master and true disciple.

Due to our own limitations, however, we think of everything in physical terms. We evaluate the master's presence and power by measures of time and space. At the satsang centres around the world, when site sevadars or local board members are called into business meetings with the master, we may imagine that this proximity to the master around the conference table brought them better concentration, more focused simran, deeper enjoyment of the Shabd. We may even think that those who are lucky enough to be Dera sevadars, residing at the Dera all year round, must have become especially evolved souls.

By virtue of this theory everyone who is initiated by a Beas master could become an evolved soul by moving to Dera! And, indeed, many of us do wish we could do just that – we think that if only we lived at the Dera our meditation would be more focused. If only we could spend our days in some physical proximity to the master, surely our soul would fly up into the higher realms. If only our circumstances were different. If only . . .

It doesn't work like that.

The master tells us he is the nearest of the near; he is with us all the time, every minute of every day, just not physically. We need to look to his presence where it is: within us. The real master, as he so often reminds us, is the Shabd within. We each have the opportunity to spend time with our master one-to-one, every day, in meditation. Through simran we can develop an awareness of the master's presence, realizing that he is with us all the time.

Unfortunately, Dera sevadars do not attain enlightenment by living in the confines of the colony, nor do those sevadars in various parts of the world who are called to frequent meetings with the master – unfortunately, because we might all wish it were that easy. We can't say or guess or even speculate about why anyone's circumstances are what they are – why some have more access to seeing the master than others.

The only thing we can say with certainty is that each of us has been placed in the precise circumstances that are in our best interest, where we can best clear our karmas, where we can live out our destiny for this life and fulfil our duties, and at the same time we can best realize our spiritual potential.

However, for those who do enjoy more frequent contact with the master than their fellow initiates, attending small meetings and interviews, this seeming privilege has its own dangers. It can inflate the ego. It can make us vulnerable to one of the spiritual seeker's most harmful diseases: the VIP Syndrome.

ILLUSION: He or she is a very important person

VIP stands for 'Very Important Person'. Would any genuine spiritual seeker dare claim that title?

A spiritual path is about losing one's identity, surrendering the ego, killing the 'I'. Spirituality does not recognize important people – rather it crushes their importance.

There is only one way to liberation, and that is to smash the mountainous ego to rubble . . . and then to grind that rubble to dust . . . and then to toss it away. The gateway to spirituality cannot accommodate boulders or big hard chunks of ego rubble. The 'I' is a mountain. Mountains cannot squeeze through the narrow entrance to the inner world.

Yet don't we all think of some initiates as more important and others as less important? Some are big, some little. Some are in high positions, some in low, unimportant positions.

We continue to think this way, even though the master says again and again that spirituality belongs to each and every person in equal measure.

Each initiate has an individual relationship with the master and with the divine. The master knows each of us better than we know ourselves. He works with each one of us individually, subtly helping and supporting each one according to our spiritual needs. Put all the master's initiates together and what do we have? The master's beloved sangat.

So long as we think of ourselves as members of an organization in which some are more important than others, we are distorting the spiritual path and creating precisely the problems associated with many religious organizations. Of course, with so large a sangat as there is today, there must be organization. Organizational matters such as delegating responsibilities, arranging meeting places for satsang or feeding and housing the large numbers of people who come together for satsang must be administered efficiently.

Yet the roles we play in the organization have nothing to do with the spiritual reality which is its purpose. What we see is the organization; but the sangat comes together to experience a spiritual reality which is more subtle and far more beautiful than the structure and appearance of the organization. The sangat comes together to share in the experience of satsang and to support one another in our search for Truth.

Let's look at the reasons we might think certain people are important. And the reasons why some initiates might even imagine themselves to be VIPs.

First: We are important if we hold a particular seva position.

Actually no seva is important or unimportant; all seva is equal. If we know that seva is a gift from the master then that is the *only* thing that makes it important.

Applying our usual worldly approach, we may look at the coordinator of a particular project or the 'in-charge' and say he or she is the 'boss'. But just as a car cannot run on three wheels, all sevas are interdependent. One seva supports the other. In the final analysis, no one is the boss, for seva is team-work. If we hold any position in seva, the focus should be on creating a harmonious, congenial team atmosphere so that the seva will go on smoothly. Self-importance has no place in any seva position.

Administration is set up to serve, not the other way around. Administrative sevadars, such as members of the board, chair-persons, representatives, have a grave responsibility to show by their actions that they consider themselves as a part of the sangat, in no way superior to or more important than any other person in the sangat.

Second: Giving donations makes us VIPs.

A donation given with a motive ceases being a donation; the so-called donation becomes a bargaining chip, as if we were in a position to haggle with the Lord. And if the motive is to see oneself as someone important in the sangat, then it's a transaction that undermines the very foundations of spirituality within the person making the donation.

Maharaj Charan Singh once spoke about a disciple with one leg who used to come to Beas to attend satsang: "He was very poor. Just to save money to give in seva, he used to walk from his village in the hills to the Dera, with the help of his crutches, covering a distance of over 75 miles. Once he was brought to me. . . . He offered one rupee in seva. Looking to his poverty, I asked the sevadars not to accept it, but he burst into tears and I had to accept his offering."

While we may think that making a very large donation makes us important, in fact the amount of any donation is irrelevant. From a spiritual point of view, the attitude with which we make a gift is all-important. Only the love with which a donation is made matters.

Third: Being seen close to the master, having access to spend time with him, makes us VIPs.

Really? Do we believe this? Unfortunately, many of us do. We see certain people who have frequent one-on-one meetings with the master and we imagine they must be very important. Maybe we even get jealous. We wish that we ourselves were the person enjoying those frequent meetings.

A Tibetan proverb says: The master is like a fire. Stand too close and you'll get burnt; stand too far and you won't get the heat.

Can close personal access to the master really 'burn' a disciple? If we're not on our guard, that very closeness can inflate the ego, bring out the judgemental aspect of the mind and destroy the very nature of the disciple-master relationship. Closeness can breed familiarity. Closeness can burn faith, burn trust, and burn love. Then the disciple ceases to be a disciple; the disciple fails to see the master as a master. The disciple burns. The disciple's faith and love go up in flames and may burn to ashes.

"Stand too far away and you won't get any heat." Another extreme. This is not about physical distance. After all, our karmas may have placed us on the opposite side of the world. Standing far away is when we disassociate ourselves from the tenets of Sant Mat, stray from the teachings, absent ourselves from satsang and do not attend to meditation. When we stray so far, we fail to feel the heat of the master's 'fire'. Then we cannot benefit from the teachings, nor can we be receptive to the master's grace.

In Great Master's words: "When we are away from the master and the satsang, the world imperceptibly impresses itself on us so much so that, in spite of our regularly giving time to simran and Nam, we often begin to feel discouraged, dry and desolate."

This is being too far from the 'fire' that is the master.

Let's aspire to follow the middle path – not so close that we burn, not so far that we don't get the heat. Let's not aspire to be VIPs, just simple disciples.

> **When we are away from the master and satsang, we often begin to feel discouraged and desolate**

7

ABOUT DARSHAN

The commonly understood meaning of the word 'darshan' is to see or look. When seekers and initiates look at the master as he sits on the dais to give satsang, we call it 'darshan'. Even if the master drives by and we catch a glimpse of him through the car window, we call it 'darshan'.

However, the present master has explained many times that someone sitting seven seas away might be enjoying darshan, while someone sitting in the front row in the satsang hall might not. What does he mean when he says that the people gazing at him from the front row might not be having darshan? After all, the master is seated right before them, in full view, and they are looking at him. And how can someone on the other side of the world, who obviously can't see him seated on the dais, be enjoying darshan? Clearly, what we think of as darshan and what the masters mean by darshan are two different things.

And so we entertain a host of illusions, such as:

ILLUSION: Being closer means better darshan

When the sangat gathers to enjoy the master's darshan, probably each initiate would like to sit as close to the dais as possible. Each one would choose to sit in the front row if the limitations of three-dimensional space would allow it! This is only natural. When we look at the master, we would like to see his features clearly. Even with 20/20 vision, our physical eyes can only do so much.

Nonetheless, the master tells us that if we believe that by sitting closer we get better darshan, this is a fallacy. In fact, this fallacy can cause unnecessary jostling for position as well as a lot of confusion, envy and hard feelings. With this belief, we restrict the master's power by thinking the master is a human body sitting on a stage, so the closer we are the better will be the darshan. We cage the master's power in the confined space of our ignorance.

The master keeps telling us that the real master is the Shabd. He asks: In which particle of the creation is the Shabd not present? He reminds us that the master is with each and every initiate every minute of the day and night, regardless of where the initiate is.

Clearly, we don't understand what darshan is. We hear the master say these things but, if we speak in terms of 'front seats' and 'back seats', we clearly do not believe him.

Physical space and mathematical measurements have nothing to do with the master's radiance; his power isn't stronger in the front of a satsang hall and weaker at the back. We only need to be receptive. The best and most effective way of making ourselves more receptive is meditation.

Day in, day out, the daily practice of meditation develops a person's receptivity. If we are not meditating, we will not be able to absorb the radiance of the master. The master's power is there in all its might; it is constantly there. If we keep attending to the meditation practice, we will grow in awareness of it. To skip meditation is like shutting our doors and closing the curtains across our windows so his radiance cannot reach us.

We need to hear the master's message that there is no substitute for meditation. He says it repeatedly, loud and clear. Just as there is no substitute for food to assuage hunger, so in cosmic law there is no substitute for meditation to connect us with the spiritual power within us. In Christ's words, "Everyone who drinks of this water [ordinary water from a well] will thirst again; but whoever drinks of the water that I will give him shall never thirst, but the water that I will give him shall be in him a well of water springing up to everlasting life."

For all our calculating, no amount of staring at the master's physical form will erase our karmas, or fulfil our spiritual needs, or substitute for meditation.

ILLUSION: Darshan on the screen is not real darshan

As the sangat has grown, satsang venues have also necessarily grown larger and larger. All around the world, there are satsang venues that are so large that people seated in the back can barely see the master. In these settings large TV screens have been installed so that anyone, seated anywhere, can see the master's face clearly as he gives satsang, answers questions, or sits giving darshan.

Many people have the illusion that looking at the master directly is 'real darshan' – even if you have to squint and he is so far away that you really can't see him – and that looking at him on the TV screen is not 'real darshan'.

Maharaj Charan Singh used to say that darshan is nothing but the helplessness of the lover to look at the beloved. In other words, it is not the looking; it is the helplessness. The helplessness to look can be equally aroused by watching the master on the screen as on the dais. It is the love that matters. If love for the master is inspired by watching him on the screen, then 'screen darshan' has been 'real darshan'.

When asked whether it is better to look directly at him or at the TV screen, which is clearer but just a 'reflection' of him, the present master pointed to himself and responded: Even this is a reflection.

If both are reflections of the reality, then what is the reality? The living master is a reflection, at the physical level, of Shabd – because Shabd itself is beyond form. He is the Formless in form. The present master's response invites us to ponder deeply on what the masters are saying to us.

ILLUSION: The more darshan we 'do', the more we 'get' from him

The present master often points out that we have very calculating minds. With our calculating nature, we approach everything with the unspoken questions: What's in it for me? What will I get out of it?

We often speak of 'getting' darshan. We turn to each other and say things like: I got a good darshan. Did you get a good darshan?

We may chase after every remotely possible opportunity to see the master, even as we cut our meditation practice short. Suppose we hear that he will drive by a particular spot on the road on his way somewhere and then he will drive by again on his way back. So we wait at that spot for hours, and after he has passed by both ways, we say: I got two darshans. As if darshan could be counted!

How many times has the master told us that we can't 'get' darshan; darshan is given. Darshan is the master's gift. No matter how we position ourselves for darshan, or how we predict the timings of his comings and goings, these types of calculations cannot make us receptive to his gift. Becoming receptive is inner work.

Maharaj Charan Singh used to say there is no calculation in love.

In fact, the calculation of hoping to 'get something' from darshan blocks the love that is the very joy of darshan.

ILLUSION: There's a right way to do darshan

It has been suggested that the way to do darshan is to focus exclusively on the master's eyes and forehead, and never ever to blink while we are looking at him. Some of us take this concept and miss the underlying point: that as love develops in us we will be helplessly drawn to gazing at our master's face.

Ultimately, the love will not let us look away or blink. Instead, we believe that the 'right way' to do darshan is to stare and stare even as our eyes get dry and need a quick blink. This kind of mechanical approach is not what darshan is all about.

In fact, once when asked about this, the present master responded: We are not zombies!

Darshan is natural. When we see a dear friend, our eyes are naturally drawn to him or her. When we are in love, we like to gaze at our beloved. We can't help it. Darshan is a natural expression of the love between master and disciple.

Love of the form is there to lead to the love of the Formless

The present master has said: The path begins with love and ends with love. The love that is the end of the spiritual path – the love of God, the love of the One, love in which we cease to exist as a separate entity – is beyond our ability even to imagine. We can't love what we can't see. We can't love something we know nothing about and have never experienced. We can't love an abstract concept. The physical form is the gateway to the spiritual journey. In his human form the master kindles the fire of love within us.

Maharaj Charan Singh wrote: "May your love of the form culminate in the love of the Formless." The present master quotes these words of Hazur Maharaj Ji again and again to keep directing us towards what is true.

8

ABOUT SATSANG

The literal meaning of 'satsang' is the company (*sang*) of truth (*sat*). When we gather for satsang, we listen to a discourse on the teachings of the saints. Hearing these teachings explained helps orient our minds to the spiritual reality the saints convey to the world – especially if we pay close attention to what is being said with the firm resolve to put it into practice. In this sense we turn toward keeping company with Truth.

However, it is the spiritual atmosphere we experience in such a gathering that matters. This uplifting atmosphere comes from the master's presence. His presence may be physical – when he is physically there at the satsang – or it may be his spiritual presence. As Maharaj Charan Singh often said when he was asked about satsang where the master is not physically there: "What makes you think I'm not there when I'm not there?"

Many of our illusions about satsang come from confusing the physical event – people gathering in a hall to hear a discourse – with the spiritual reality. With this confusion, we start to believe that . . .

ILLUSION: Attending satsang is mandatory

We all have been in schools where attending class is compulsory; we also have belonged to social, political or religious societies where attendance at meetings or participation in public observances is required. So it is only natural that we carry this idea over into satsang.

The masters frequently stress that there is no ritual or ceremony about satsang. We do not establish our reputation as a 'good satsangi' by regular attendance at satsang – and by making sure others see that we are dutifully present. Nor do we gain any spiritual merit simply by showing up and marking our presence at satsang.

How easy it is to slip into taking satsang attendance as a routine. The mind just relishes routine!

Do we just show up at satsang, much as we would attend church or visit the gurdwara or go to the mosque at the regular times set by the religion we belong to? Do we treat it as a ceremony, which as members of a community we must attend? Do we fear that others will judge us as 'bad satsangis' if we don't attend satsang regularly? Do we even judge others who don't attend satsang regularly as being less committed to the spiritual path?

Satsang can be a great help to any initiate striving to keep his focus on the spiritual purpose of his life. It can be an invaluable source of strength for each of us struggling to sustain our efforts on the path amidst a world of distracting influences.

If, however, we slip into thinking of satsang as a communal ritual, a ceremonial observance that is mandatory for our 'membership', we are missing the point.

ILLUSION: Attending satsang is enough

The masters keep explaining that satsang is not an end in itself; rather, it is a support to meditation. Do we think we can skip meditation, or cut it short, because we went to satsang today? After all, there are only so many hours in a day.

Great Master used to liken satsang to a fence around a crop. Just as any crop without a fence is vulnerable, so our 'crop' of meditation needs the protective 'fence' of regular satsang. The atmosphere of satsang, he would say, helps us think clearly about our priorities and the purpose of our lives. Without satsang, the desires and ambitions, the worries and cares, the regrets and frustrations that continually pull our attention away from the spiritual focus are like the animals that may steal into a garden that has no fence and take away the crop.

In Great Master's analogy of satsang being like a fence around the crop, it is the crop that is important. Can a fence replace the crop? The fence is to protect something. What is the point of a fence around an empty field?

The present master has often likened satsang to an appetizer. When we dine at a fine restaurant, the appetizer is a small, delicious titbit that precedes the meal. This tasty morsel whets the appetite, wakes up the taste buds, so that we're ready to fully enjoy the meal. Satsang, he says, is just such an appetizer, whetting our appetite for meditation. The atmosphere of satsang gives us a taste – a flavour of spiritual truth – so that we desire more of that delectable flavour.

Enter satsang and the mind can settle, centred in a place of peace and stillness and clarity – at least temporarily. We get a taste of something, and we want more. We might call that something 'home'; we might call it 'love'. Something deep inside us recognizes our direction.

In the atmosphere of satsang we can be reminded of our true identity, and for a moment all the empty trappings of our worldly identity fade into the shadows. Whether we are politicians, professionals, industrialists, farmers – whether we're young or old, fat or thin, man or woman, rich or poor, beautiful or scarred, whether we have one limb or four – to the master we are soul. In the master's eyes, we are all beautiful, all full of light, all equal. We are all loved. In the atmosphere of his presence, we may get a fleeting glimpse of ourselves in his eyes. And the consuming hunger that drew us to the saints' teachings in the first place is roused.

While satsang may whet the appetite – giving us just a small taste of the real 'food' we hunger after – meditation is the only place where that appetite can be satisfied.

ILLUSION: Satsangs should be entertaining so they engage us

In satsang the same teachings are repeated. And repeated. And repeated. And so we complain that the discourses are too repetitive. They do not engage us.

The fact is, the mystic message doesn't change. The teachings are simple and straightforward and there is only one message to give. It can only be repeated.

It is we who continually lose focus. We drift away from the focal point and the purpose of our lives. The repetition brings us back to the focus. Again and again we are reminded of our goal. Slowly and slowly, the repetition gives us a solid preparation for meditation.

If we are receptive, just one word in a discourse may change our thinking and attitude. Just one line in a satsang may turn our lives around. Even if we absorb one word or one line in a satsang, it has served its purpose.

However, we need to be open; we need to be ready to learn and absorb. It is our own need that brings us to satsang.

———

There was once a seeker who went to a master and asked for instruction in Truth. The master very simply said, "Everything is Consciousness and thou art that. That is Truth."

"Is that all?" the seeker asked. "Can't you elaborate some more?"
"That's all I have to teach. If you want something else, you will have to find another master."

Disappointed, the seeker left and eventually found his way to another master who had a large ashram and many disciples. The seeker asked the new master, "I want to know Truth. Please instruct me."

With a glance, the master understood what kind of seeker he was. "Have you been to another master?" he asked.

"Oh yes," said the seeker, "but he couldn't instruct me on Truth."

"All right, I will give you the instruction. But first you will have to serve me for twelve years without question. We need someone to pick up the cow dung. Are you willing to do that?"

"Yes," said the seeker enthusiastically. And he was taken into the ashram. At the end of twelve years, he said to the master, "Twelve years are over. Please instruct me on Truth."

"Very good," said the master. "Here is my teaching: Everything is Consciousness and thou art that."

Bewildered, the seeker said, "But that is exactly what the other master told me."

"Of course," replied the Master, "Truth hasn't changed in twelve years and never will."

"But why did I have to spend twelve years picking up cow dung?" asked the seeker.

The master replied, "Because your mind was too clogged to understand. The master has only to say one word, and if the disciple is open and ready to hear, then Truth will explode within the disciple."

———

Our minds are clogged. We need to be attentive, open and receptive. Attending satsang can help clear those blockages. Satsang can inspire us to move in the direction where Truth will explode within us.

ILLUSION: Some satsangs are 'good', some are 'bad'

The master frequently tells us there are no good or bad satsangs. Yet each one of us may find ourselves saying, "Wow!

That was a great satsang!" Or, "That satsang just didn't hold my attention; it was boring." Indeed it seems to be a common experience that some satsangs are uplifting and others leave us flat.

To understand this seeming contradiction between the master's words and our experience, we need first to distinguish between 'satsang' and 'discourse'. Satsang is something far subtler and more powerful than any discourse. No matter how eloquent or clear or inspiring the words of the speaker, the discourse is not the satsang. The discourse is only an activity that occurs during satsang.

Clearly, some speakers may be more skilled orators than others; some may have a more pleasing voice; some may have a way with words. But we don't come to satsang to hear words cleverly put together. Nor do we come to satsang for its entertainment value.

If we understand 'satsang' to mean the company of Truth, we know why we come to satsang. And if we come to satsang with the intention and the focus to open ourselves to the experience of satsang, then we'll find that every discourse is 'good'. Very good, indeed!

From the perspective of the speaker, of course, the above cannot be taken as an excuse to shirk the responsibility of the seva. The seva of speaking at satsang means putting time, effort and focused attention into preparing the discourse.

On the other hand, from our perspective as listeners at satsang, our own seva is to be open and receptive to the atmosphere of the master's presence and to the truth of the teachings – sometimes even in spite of the failings of the speaker. This is an important seva and a significant discipline of the path of the masters. Going to satsang becomes an act of devotion. Meditation becomes an act of love. We cannot reach love without devotion, and therefore satsang comes first and then love is born.

In the many satsangs around the world where the master is not physically present, the atmosphere of the master's presence is invoked by the focus and intention of all those who attend. Every member of the gathered sangat has an equal part in invoking the master's presence through simran, focus, love and the clear intention to be in satsang – in the company of Truth. Speaker and congregation, every single person is equally a part of it!

As Christ said, "For where two or three have gathered together in my name, there am I in their midst," and Great Master similarly said, "Where two or more satsangis are gathered to discuss Sant Mat, the Sat Guru is also there." In other words, true satsang in all its profundity can happen when two people sit down on the side of the road to discuss the master and his teachings. Equally, it can happen when hundreds or thousands gather in a satsang hall to hear a formal discourse.

Great Master wrote: "When a particular subject is discussed in satsang all the listeners think of the same subject simultaneously, with the result that the entire environment is saturated with their thought currents. The entire audience benefits thereby, and the subject leaves an indelible impression on the minds of those present." In other words, it is the fact that all the listeners' thought currents are focused on the truths being discussed which charges the atmosphere with significance and benefits all the listeners in proportion to the focus of their attention.

One of the dangers in thinking in terms of good and bad satsangs is that we may start to imagine that a speaker whose discourses delight us is spiritually evolved. We might imagine that the uplift we felt during their discourse was due to the speaker and his or her words. With that kind of thinking we're on our way to creating a priestly class. And we're missing the point of satsang.

ILLUSION: Satsang speakers are elevated souls

Are speakers selected for the seva of giving satsang because they are spiritually advanced? Some of us actually have this misconception about satsang speakers.

In fact, speakers are not chosen because they are considered more knowledgeable about the saints' teachings, nor because they are thought to be more spiritually elevated. Satsang speakers may be selected because they have some skill in public speaking, much as a farmer might be given the seva of planting a field – a seva that a city dweller would have no idea how to do. Satsang speakers are selected because they are able to express themselves in a way that others can easily understand. But that's a very different thing from spiritual elevation.

The knowledge of a speaker comes from listening to satsangs and from books; they repeat the teachings from the masters' discourses, from other satsangs, or by reading spiritual literature. Speakers are ordinary sevadars. They are struggling as much as anyone else.

As a matter of fact, doing the seva of speaking might be the best way to crush the ego for a speaker. The challenge of sitting before the sangat explaining the high principles of Sant Mat, knowing full well that one is speaking to people whose attainment may be much higher than one's own, might be just the thing to humble that troublesome ego.

Being a satsang speaker can, however, make us vulnerable to a false sense of our personal importance. Buoyed up by the sangat's loving attention as we speak, we can get confused. We could even start to think the atmosphere of love and inspiration that fills the sangat hall comes from our words. Or worse, from our imagined spiritual accomplishments.

Ego is subtle; ego is powerful; ego is ubiquitous, affecting every one of us. It is possible that as speakers we might start to imagine we have been selected as a channel for the master's true teachings because we are specially gifted and enjoy a lofty spiritual station. If this happens, we are suffering a serious delusion.

Only one who has embodied Truth can be a true preacher, a teacher of Truth. Only he can teach true spirituality who is all-knowing – and that is the master. The fragrance of Truth permeates the master's words and seekers after Truth are automatically drawn to that sweet scent. Some of the early Sufi masters used to say that a saint was like the perfume of God on earth. They said it was the fragrance of this perfume that reached the heart of a seeker, arousing a deep longing for God.

The masters' satsangs are the highest form of teachings; they are invaluable and authentic. Through the masters' discourses we get indisputable learning, inspiration and motivation. The master expresses Truth with the authority of real knowledge from real experience. The master is the teachings personified.

If we start thinking of speakers – or of any sevadars serving in any capacity – as being more spiritually evolved than others, we are confusing outward, visible shows of life with inner reality. We are confusing spirituality with the roles played in an organization. We are confusing the sevadar with the One being served.

Spirituality belongs
to each and every person
in equal measure

9

ABOUT SEVA

Seva means selfless service, given freely, service given out of love with no thought of reward. Doing seva is easy for those who want to give. Doing seva is difficult for those who want to get.

Seva is a silent offering of our devotion to the master. It has been said that work done as seva is love made visible. In this sense seva is a way of expressing our devotion. A task can only be said to be seva when we serve without ego or pride, without expectation for any gain. Without humility, there is no seva.

Most of us, however, are locked in a self-centred state where 'I', 'me' and 'mine' drive whatever we do. Therefore, the seva we do can only be our *effort* to surrender and humble our egos. We start from where we are. Through seva, we go through a learning and cleansing process to expand our horizons and become more aware.

Seva gives us precious, though sometimes painful, opportunities to recognize and realize our flaws, faults and shortcomings. Any seva we are given – no matter what it is – is a great and precious gift. It is a gift to be treasured, though we may not know why this gift has been placed before us.

Once there was a wealthy young man who became a disciple of a Sufi sheikh. At the sheikh's *khanqah* or gathering place, he was given the task of cleaning the toilets. His mother, who was a famous physician, felt this was inappropriate for her son and sent twelve of her slaves to the sheikh with instructions that they should be used to clean the toilets. The sheikh wrote to her: You are a physician. If your son had an inflammation of the gall bladder, would you want me to give the needed medicine to the slaves, or to him?

Seva is the needed medicine for the disease that sickens all of us: ego. If we become intensely absorbed in serving, we just may forget the self. When we begin to discard or disregard the self, the task we are doing begins to be seva. We might not even be conscious that this transformation is taking place because we are so absorbed in our service.

What are some of the illusions we have about seva?

ILLUSION: Physical seva can replace meditation

Into the rare opportunity of seva that the master gives us, we bring our own calculations: if we do seva, we think, we do not need to do meditation. We calculate that if we spend so many hours in seva, surely it must replace the need for meditation for that day. We reason that we always fail at meditation. Surely, we say to ourselves, we are unable to meditate. However, we are quite able to sweep or to build, or to cook or to manage a computer system. Therefore it seems quite logical to us that if we serve the sangat with the skills we do have, then we can skip the skill we apparently do not have: meditation.

The master repeatedly explains that the purpose of seva is to support meditation. The highest seva is meditation itself.

> **The purpose of seva is to support meditation**

Physical or outer seva helps to create the right frame of mind for attending to meditation. It is a means, not an end. There is no substitute for the inner service of meditation.

ILLUSION: No common sense is required in seva

Sometimes in seva we think the master's power and grace will make everything work out. Who needs common sense?

At satsang centres around the world, where sevadars engage in rigorous and challenging construction tasks, many sevadars believe that no safety precautions are required. Because they are doing the master's seva, they believe he will protect them. Just to take a particularly extreme example of this type of thinking, sevadars working on a roof or high scaffolding refuse to use safety harnesses or wear helmets. Sevadars working with power tools or toxic chemicals refuse to wear safety goggles or proper gloves. They say the master's protection is all they need.

Is this an inspiring example of trust in the divine power of the master, or an illusion?

Actually, serious problems arise out of this misconception: sevadars have been injured while doing seva. Moreover, the sevadar who believed that the master's power was supposed to protect him or her from physical injury may lose faith in the master's path.

Rumi related a story to illustrate the correct way of trusting in the divine: A man asked the Prophet whether it is better to shackle his camel's legs or to trust in God. It would be normal, of course, to shackle the camel's legs before going to sleep lest the camel would wander too far in the night. Yet, the man wondered, if he shackled his camel's legs, did this show a lack of trust in God?

The Prophet answered: First shackle your camel's legs and then trust in God. That is, even if one uses common sense and shackles the camel's legs, problems may still arise beyond one's control: camel thieves may come; the camel may break free; the camel may sicken and die. One still needs to have trust in God and lay worries aside. But if one does not follow the precautions dictated by common sense first, then one is only avoiding responsibility.

Once, when asked about sevadars who claim that the master's grace would protect them and refuse to follow safety precautions, the present master called this way of thinking very foolish, even bordering on lunacy. Such a person might as well stand in front of an oncoming truck, he said, and expect the master to protect him. He said: They must use proper safety equipment. They must. There are much better uses for the master's grace than that.

ILLUSION: The tangible rewards of seva matter

At the Dera and at satsang centres around the world, sevadars often wear badges, making it easy to identify where they are working and what their job is.

In some of the large satsang centres, however, the sevadars' badges may also indicate that the sevadar is free to observe a different protocol from the majority of the sangat. For example, when the master visits the centre, there may be scheduled times of satsang when the general sangat is welcome to attend, and other times when only authorized sevadars, those with badges denoting a specific role, are allowed onsite. Some of us who wait in hotels or in a nearby town while the centre is closed to the general sangat may well think of those lucky souls with sevadar badges as a privileged group. We may long for a badge so we too can be near the master, or see him walk by as he checks the arrangements for satsang.

So what happens? Do we then want to do seva primarily to get a sevadar's badge? Perhaps we also do wish to serve; perhaps we would even be happy to do any menial task; yet our motivation is not pure and unalloyed. We want that sevadar badge! Does the badge make us feel special? Does it make us feel important? Approaching seva with this attitude obviously runs counter to the very purpose of doing seva.

Similarly, the master sometimes expresses his gratitude for the dedicated hard work done by sevadars by giving them parshad. Sevadars' parshad, then, offers the calculating mind another opportunity to distort the purpose and nature of seva. Do we want to do seva so we can get sevadars' parshad? Seva is about giving, not getting.

If we approach seva with the idea of getting anything – whether it is a badge, parshad, prestige, close physical proximity to the master, power or recognition – we negate the seva even as we do it. This is what the calculating mind does: it takes the opportunity of seva that the master provides and twists it into its very opposite by using it to try to get adornments for 'me'.

Happily for us all, the calculating mind is less powerful than the living master. It may be sneaky in its devious ways, but the master too has his ways to bring even the most arrogant and self-serving of us around – slowly and slowly – to true discipleship.

ILLUSION: Certain seva positions confer power and prestige

'Self-serving' and 'sevadar' are two mutually exclusive concepts. If we are self-serving, we are not sevadars. If we are sevadars, we are not self-serving.

Yet how easy it is for us to fall into thinking that having a seva task carries with it a certain prestige and power. We may think that because we are the coordinator of a project it must mean that we are more important than the masses of sevadars working on the project. If our seva puts us in the public limelight, we may be tempted to take a little secret pleasure from the fact that people know our name and think we're important.

How easily we can be deluded into thinking our seva post allows us to be inconsiderate or push others around. Naturally, when we adopt such attitudes it not only undoes our seva, but also makes it difficult for others doing seva with us. And can we really think that with such an attitude we are serving our all-loving, all-compassionate master?

Do we think that a seva position with a big title is more valuable in the master's eyes than seva that goes unrecognized in the sangat? Think of the many sevadars who are working on various projects in the far corners of the world. In today's high-tech world, they may be working on a database or doing editing or reviewing books for the Dera Library. They do their seva alone in the quiet of their own home. They have no recognition; no one knows what they are doing. Living at such a distance from the Dera, they rarely have the darshan of the master. Yet they persevere, devoting long hours to the task, year after year, even decade after decade.

Who can put a value on any particular seva? Who can say what is important or unimportant?

Think of the sevadars doing *luk* seva (road resurfacing). At the very hottest time of the year, when the steaming asphalt is softest, they work out in the blazing sun all day. They don't complain about the weather or the lack of fans. They don't look for cold water to quench their thirst, nor comfortable chairs and better accommodation. They are *mast*, intoxicated with seva, blissfully happy, completely absorbed and content in what they are doing.

All seva is equal. It's not even useful or appropriate to compare one seva to another.

If any seva is assigned to us – whether being a representative or sweeping the grounds – what levels of spiritual accomplishment are needed to do the seva asked of us? Great

Master made the true situation amply clear when he said that if the master wants, he can get his seva done even by a stone.

Doing seva – whether under the blazing sun or seated in an air-conditioned office, whether in full view where lots of people know what we're doing or out of sight in a place far from Dera – it is all the same. A seva position is neither important nor unimportant. It is an opportunity to serve. It is an opportunity to become so engrossed, committed and involved in serving the Lord that nothing else matters.

A unique reward of seva is that we imbibe the qualities of the one we serve

The masters repeatedly stress that in seva we should work collectively, shoulder to shoulder, irrespective of caste, creed, colour and social status. In seva there is no king or pauper, no senior or junior, no official or labourer. In the master's ocean of love, there is place only for the unconditional, helpless, humble, surrendering soul! In seva we find a place where rank and position don't matter, where promotion and recognition are irrelevant, where the only thing that matters is our humanity, devotion, love and obedience.

We may recall how boldly and fearlessly the master wiped out class distinction at the langar. When Maharaj Charan Singh first became the master, he found that caste prejudice was still practised in the langar. In spite of the fact that the masters had always taught that the soul has no distinctions and that we all are children of the one Lord, the sangat was not able to rise above these deep-rooted prejudices. People who came from the lower segments of society were still segregated from the rest of the sangat. Speaking at sat-sang, the master advised the sangat to give up their preju-dices and eat together as brothers and sisters. Several people in the administration warned him that his stance was too radical, that people would not be able to accept such a chal-lenge to their long-standing prejudices. The next day, when the master visited the langar, he found that those from the most marginalized communities were huddled together, sep-arate from the rest. The master sat down among them and ate his lunch. And since that day, the langar has been free of social divisions.

This is our true inheritance; this is part of the greatness of character we have to imbibe from the master. Great Master wrote: "Seva has many rewards, but the unique one is that a person imbibes the qualities of the person he serves!"

The masters set a noble benchmark for us. Their example can be our goal – to be supremely, magnificently human, to practise human equality, and to serve without expectation, ego or pride.

ILLUSION: Seva needs us

There's a subtlety about seva that often eludes our materi-alistic mindset. We are accustomed to working in our jobs, serving in our communities, doing chores for our families. In these settings, if we were suddenly to stop doing our duty, there would be a gap. The work would stop. We must keep working, and we *do* keep working, because we know we are needed. The work matters; in fact, we matter. It's just the way things are in the world.

So we bring this same way of thinking to seva. But seva doesn't work like that. Actually, in seva none of us is indispensable, and the master's work will not come to a grinding halt because of our absence. The master's work is liberation of our soul.

The master's work is divine work, spiritual work – not an earthly or physical activity. All the master does, and all he gets done by us, is for the one purpose of freeing us from the darkness of ignorance we live in. His concern is not the outward manifestations of the inner work he is doing. He is only concerned with the extent to which the outer work is furthering liberation from our petty, limited, egotistical selves. He can do his work in whatever way he decides.

We may think that a particular seva was given to us because we are so talented or smart or educated, or even because we are so diplomatic or humble. We pride ourselves on the virtues we believe we have. However, in many cases we cannot even guess why a particular seva is given to a particular person. Dera has been known to have a vice-chancellor of a university do seva in the Dera fruit stall. At the Dera and at centres around the world, people from all walks of life are doing all kinds of seva. Doctors are doing *mitti seva* (earth moving for building works), government officials are serving food, army officers are washing dishes in the kitchens. Teachers and professors are scrubbing toilets. Judges and lawyers stand in the parking lots guiding the traffic.

Seva is a gift to us from the master, given as per the need of the particular sevadar as only the master knows. But what it is the master sees – that is a mystery to us.

We mistake what is going on and think our work and our activities are important. If we have a particular seva task to do, we may believe the task couldn't get done without us, or that it couldn't be done properly. If we have responsibility for some large or complex project, we may even secretly believe our project, department or satsang centre would fall apart without us. However, we can be transferred, retired, resign, or die, and the project, department or satsang centre will go on without a break for just as long as the master wants it to go on.

There is an evocative saying about seva that is often quoted by members of the sangat: *Seva keetyaan mukhti nahin. Na keetyaan, rukhti nahin.* By doing seva, seva doesn't get finished. By not doing it, it doesn't stop.

This brief, pithy aphorism says that if we do seva, it will nonetheless never run out; it will go on and on – it will never finish. On the other hand, even if we don't do seva, it will go right on too; it will go on and continue without us.

Seva, true seva, is the Lord's love in action on earth, a love that is the very life force of the creation. Without that love, creation would not exist. If we give ourselves to seva, the seva will just keep coming and coming. Like a river it will keep flowing. And we will be in that river, a river of grace. If we stop doing seva, we will not be missed. The seva will go on. The river will continue to flow.

As the present master puts it: We need seva; seva doesn't need us.

Seva is the Lord's precious gift to us, so we can grow in his love. We can value it in this light. It is not ours because we want it. It is not ours because we are fit for it. It is not ours because we are suited to it, or we deserve it. As long as it is in our destiny to do the Lord's work, we will find we have the strength, brains, energy and health to do it. Equally, we can lose it all in a flash with a stroke, brain haemorrhage, Alzheimer's, or some major change in life circumstances – in so many ways!

In seva, we are nobodies. This is not just a figure of speech. Nor is it a decree that we 'should' be nobodies. It is a fact, one that becomes abundantly clear as we actually do seva. We don't have the capacity to do seva on our own. Seva is done when we lose ourselves in that river of grace that is the Lord's love. We may not recognize this at first, but seva will teach us this fact.

The ocean does not dry up if a drop or ripple spills onto the shore. Our contribution as individuals is negligible, inconsequential and insignificant. For what can one little drop of water do when faced with the vast and endless expanse of the ocean? The power lies in the wholeness of the ocean, not in the individual drop. During seva we are given the opportunity to rejoice in being a part of the ocean by working together in harmony and joy. Our strength lies in the unity, the wholeness of the ocean, not in the individual drop.

10

ABOUT MEDITATION

The masters have told us in so many ways that our daily meditation practice is the single most important thing we do. As Maharaj Charan Singh put it: "My only advice is that whatever we may do and in whatever circumstances we may live, our meditation should be our main concern, and this should never be sacrificed to anything of this life."

Yet we find this advice difficult to follow. We have so many other duties and ambitions in life, and meditation seems dry and tasteless. We doubt its efficacy. Although we believe we are trying very hard, we seem not to be accomplishing anything.

So we say that meditation is very difficult. The present master, on the other hand, often says: What's so difficult about meditation? He has even said: The main thing is to enjoy your meditation. Make meditation your friend. Make it your support.

He says: Just sit down, start your simran and let go. What is so difficult about that? And when asked what we are to let go of, he answers: Let go of your self.

Let's consider the illusions that keep us tied up in knots, making meditation difficult and unenjoyable.

ILLUSION: We must make progress ... now!

Many of us want to measure our spiritual progress. Applying a mindset familiar from our worldly activities, we look for some kind of score card. Meditation doesn't work that way. We are not able to measure progress and it is not our job. We have been told simply to meditate – just that – no expectations, no rewards, no scores. Just sit every single day.

Soami Ji put the case clearly and unequivocally: "The fruit of worldly actions is quite manifest to the *jeeva* [living being] and hence he is easily entangled in the world. But the fruit of *parmarth* [spiritual work] is hidden, and belief in its value is therefore slow to develop."

We are accustomed to seeing the results of whatever we do in the world. Seeing those results keeps us engaged and involved in our worldly duties; we know we have to do our duty in the world so that the results of our efforts will be realized. So we approach meditation thinking: The more effort I put in, the more results I should see. But, as Soami Ji says, we can't see the results of spiritual work. There may be visible results, or there may not – we don't know.

Some of us seem not only to expect results, but we want those results instantly. Initiation today, enlightenment tomorrow! On this lifelong path where efforts are seemingly disconnected from any visible results, this attitude is sure to bring us a crushing disappointment.

Why do so many of us complain that we can't meditate?

The master tells us to 'meditate' and we interpret it as 'become enlightened' or 'reach the goal'. When we claim we can't meditate, all we may be saying is that we are not getting enlightened. But the master only said to attend to meditation. Clearly, we *can* sit down, close our eyes, relax and repeat simran. And when the mind runs out and we realize that we're thinking about other things, we *can* start simran again. Every single one of us *can* do this. It is called practising meditation.

How many of us actually give up in despair, feeling that we can't meditate? How many of us beg the master to shower his grace on us because we 'can't meditate'?

The present master has often told the story of a man who prayed to the Lord to let him win the lottery. Day after day, the man prayed, "O Lord, please let me win the lottery!" Finally, the Lord had to respond, "My good man, at least go out and buy yourself a lottery ticket."

ILLUSION: Progress means light and sound

Not only do we approach meditation expecting results, but we also believe we know what those results should be like. Spiritual progress, we believe, is seeing inner lights and hearing the divine melody; and if that's not happening, we decide we are failing at meditation. And all too often we get discouraged. We may even give up on meditation, figuring it must be for other people but not for us.

There's a story that the devil once decided to sell off some of his old tools. A man stopped by to see what was for sale. There were lots of fancy, shiny, complicated gadgets. But way down at the bottom of the pile was one little wedge-shaped thing. It was a dull brown and didn't look like much of anything, so the man went over to the devil and asked what it was. The devil said, "Oh no, I can't sell that one. It's my best tool. I just can't do without it! It's called discouragement."

The problem with looking for spiritual progress is that it presupposes that we know what spiritual progress looks like. Do we, in fact, know what it looks like? If we were experiencing spiritual progress would we recognize it?

There's a well-known story of a man who prayed with great devotion, "O Lord, where art thou?" He prayed fervently, hour after hour, day after day, lost in the intensity of his repetition, "O Lord, where art thou?" The devil saw that the man was becoming steeped in divine love and figured he had to do something about it. So he went to the man and said, "O you fool, for all these years you've been saying, 'O Lord, where art thou?' Has anyone ever answered you?"

The man thought about it and realized that he had never heard an answer. Discouraged and desolate, he gave up his praying. What was the point, after all? Without the bliss of his praying he fell into a deep sadness. Then the Lord spoke to him saying, "Don't you realize that your 'Where art thou?' is my 'Here I am'?"

Do we realize that our simple adherence to the practice of meditation, day after day, is the clearest evidence of the Lord pulling us into his orbit?

The present master has said: Everyone's experience will be different because their approach is different. We cannot generalize. Remember the story of the blindfolded men who are asked to touch an elephant and identify what it is! They all claim it to be something different.

When initiates have complained that they don't see any lights or hear any sounds in their meditation, the present master has responded in a light vein: You want lights and sounds? Go to a discotheque! There are plenty of lights and sounds there.

We may not see any progress simply because we are looking in the wrong direction. The thing we're looking for might be right in plain view, but we can't see it.

Are we by any chance becoming a little more aware of our weaknesses? Isn't this progress? The very thing that we used to consider our strength, we can now see clearly for what it is: a flaw. Are we becoming a little more contented, or a little happier and at peace with ourselves? Perhaps worries and cares that used to overwhelm us now seem to be manageable as we develop trust in the master. Isn't this progress?

The power of daily meditation is inexpressible for those who practise it. Slowly and gradually we do feel the sea change within. Meditation stabilizes the mind and prepares us to face adversities and calamities with courage and strength and clarity. Whether we give daily time to meditation or not, we will continue to suffer life's adversities, but those who put in the two and a half hours daily in the meditation practice can, while going through adversities, find clarity and peace of mind slowly replacing confusion and agitation.

Is that not spiritual progress?

ILLUSION: Bhajan is not essential to meditation

Many initiates live with the illusion that there's no point in attending to bhajan, that is, listening to or for the divine sound. We attend faithfully to simran, our repetition practice, but when the time comes to turn the attention to listen for the Shabd, we think: why bother? We reason that since we don't hear anything significant, what's the point in sitting there doing nothing? At least in simran we are doing something. We are repeating words. But listening for a sound that we don't hear feels a lot like doing nothing at all. But the fact is, we are not doing nothing. We are being receptive, attentive. In bhajan all our energy is given over to listening.

The present master has likened attending to bhajan to opening a shop. He has said that a shopkeeper opens his shop and waits; that way he is there when the customer arrives. If the shopkeeper were to keep the shop closed and plan only to open it when a customer actually arrives, he would never do any business.

Similarly, by attuning ourselves to the silence and practising being attentive, we 'open the shop'. We are ready and waiting for the Shabd to come into our consciousness. In fact, the Shabd is there already, resounding twenty-four hours a day. We don't hear it because our attention is elsewhere. In bhajan we simply try to train our attention in the direction of the Shabd. We train it to be attentive. And we wait. We wait attentively.

When initiates have said they don't bother with bhajan because they don't hear anything, the present master has said that this is like preparing a meal and then not eating the food. Day after day, if we attend to simran and don't do the bhajan, we deny ourselves the life-giving sustenance that this food alone can provide.

ILLUSION: Meditation is about getting results

Great Master wrote, "Service is of four kinds: with body, mind, wealth, and soul. Of these, service with the soul is the best." Meditation is service with the soul.

If we recognize that meditation is a form of service, a form of seva, we may be able to let go of any idea of 'getting' something out of it. Like any other seva, meditation is an opportunity for selfless service, service freely given in a spirit of love and without any expectation of reward. If we approach meditation in this way, the idea of getting results from it becomes meaningless. And that will help us to experience the practice of meditation as utterly enjoyable.

The present master was asked: What does meditation mean to you? He said: To me, meditation means my master. If I am doing what my master has asked me to do, and if I am pleasing him, then what more could I want?

If we approach meditation not as a way to get enlightenment but only as a way to serve and please the master who has given us so much, we will find it easier to enjoy meditation. We will be in the right frame of mind to let go. When we finally stop conceptualizing about what meditation is supposed to lead to, we can then open our minds and hearts to what is. Not what we think, not what we believe, not what we want, but just what is.

And then, just possibly, we will see beyond the prison walls of concepts and illusions where we have been trapped for so long.

11

ABOUT THE MASTER

It has been said that if all the seas were ink and all the land was paper and all the trees in the world were pens, you still couldn't write a description of the master. To understand who the master is and what he does for us is beyond the ability of words to describe. Whether we call him a friend, a teacher, a saint or God himself – these are all concepts. We can discuss them, we can heap long lists of adjectives on them, we can even argue heatedly about them – but the fact remains: they're only concepts. If we want to understand the master and his role in our lives we will have to go to a higher level of consciousness.

Meanwhile, we like to fill in the blanks with our own illusions . . . such as:

ILLUSION: The master just waves a magic wand

When we say something like "the master is God" we get ourselves into trouble. Images and concepts about God, or about the gods, learned from the various religious traditions we come from, suddenly come into play. Just listen to any question and answer session. We really do seem to think the master has come down from heaven to wave a magic wand so we can have our worldly desires granted and live happily ever after.

Do we really think that the master is here to make us live forever, to protect us from sickness and death, to make us rich, to ensure we don't meet a car accident, or to advise us on our business affairs? We seem to expect that the master will serve in our lives as a magician, doctor, stockbroker, marriage counsellor and astrologer all rolled into one.

The idea that the master is here to arrange pleasant and pain-free situations in the lives of his disciples adds all sorts of complexity and anguish to an initiate's life. As if testing the master's power to grant our wishes, we first put him on a pedestal and call him all-powerful, the greatest of the great. Then, when we are disillusioned, we drag him down from the same pedestal. When life is pleasant and rosy, we feel he is with us and take delight in his kindness and compassion, but life is not always pleasant or rosy. So it's like riding on a ferris wheel: up, up, up we go, and over the top – then down, down, down we go. Round and round! First we think he is so compassionate, then we say he doesn't care; first he is kind, then unkind; first great, then small.

We even love to attach miracles to the master if our loved one is saved in an accident. What about the other person who died? Was the master partial to one and not to the other? Which was the real miracle – for the one who died, or the one who survived?

Actually, the master is very clear and leaves no ambiguity. He does not guarantee that we will not face death, pain and other calamities. As a matter of fact, he constantly reminds us to prepare for that very death we dread so much. He reminds us that our destiny for this life is fixed as a result of our karmas. The spiritual master is not a magician, doctor, stockbroker, marriage counsellor or astrologer. He is a spiritual guide.

By doing the daily meditation practice, repeating simran during the day, and following the instructions given to us at the time of initiation, we slowly and gradually develop a level of equanimity that enables us to go through the ups and downs of life without losing our balance. Peace of mind and confidence come from the practice. The understanding dawns that whatever is happening is just the unfolding of our own karmic account. Slowly and gradually, an appreciation of the master's ever-present support grows within us.

We may go through great challenges in life. We may face truly painful circumstances. Yet, if we remain steadfast in our spiritual practice, we may be able to maintain our inner peace – notwithstanding the pain. We may even develop a growing awareness that the Lord's grace is sustaining us through our troubles.

There are two different ways of asking the master to 'wave his magic wand': one is to beg him to change the circumstances of our lives; the other is to be obedient to his instructions. By complaining and pleading with him to change the circumstances of our lives, we remain miserable. Why? Because the circumstances are not going to change. And we also weaken our own will power.

By simply obeying our master's instructions and taking action, we gradually become aware of that divine presence that supports us through all the circumstances of our lives – the good times and the bad times. We then acquire a kind of happiness and peace of mind that will seem more powerful than any 'magic wand'.

ILLUSION: The master does it all

Masquerading as a state of awe and appreciation, this misconception often serves as an excuse to avoid our personal responsibility. If you listen to any question and answer session with the master, you'll hear how many of us beg him, "Master, I can't meditate, please give me your grace. I need your *daya*, your mercy, I need your *mehr*, your grace. I truly can't meditate."

Many of us seem to firmly believe – or desperately hope – that the master in his kindness and compassion will do the meditation for us. After all, we think, he is so powerful and so gracious, and we are so weak. Surely, if any spiritual progress is going to happen, it can only be by his grace. Most certainly, he 'does it all'.

The masters explain that just as a bird flies with two wings, so also will our consciousness rise in meditation with the help of two 'wings': our effort and his grace. Our part in expanding our consciousness is to put in the best effort we are capable of.

Would we believe a bird can fly with only one wing?

Maharaj Charan Singh used to give the analogy that the Lord provides the hunger, and the Lord provides the food on the plate, but then we want the Lord to also move the fork to our mouth for us. The present master has revised this analogy. He says that now we even want the Lord to move our jaw and chew for us!

When we beg the master – "I can't meditate; give me your grace" – we show clearly that we have no idea what grace is.

Do we really think grace is something that the master gives to the person who begs the loudest, leaving others who struggle along in silence dry and desolate? The Lord's grace and mercy are flowing in abundance all the time. As Great Master put it: "The current of his mercy is flowing everywhere. It is taking care of us of itself. It knows what is for our good. It is present everywhere. It perceives our feelings and hears us."

The master is the supreme vessel and channel for mercy, love and compassion. It is his nature to give and give and give. Grace flows through him all the time to all who are ready to receive it.

The problem is not with the grace the Lord is showering but with our ability to receive. Our hearts are not open; our minds are not receptive. They are filled with worries, preoccupations and plans. Even when there's nothing particular to think about, our minds go right on generating a stream of meaningless thoughts.

When the heart is open and the mind is still and receptive, then the Lord's grace flows into and through and all around us, enlivening our life and our spiritual practice, and drawing us into the magnetic pull of that supreme love.

Ironically, disciples who do spend two and a half hours daily practising meditation and do their best to live the Sant Mat way of life will also say, "He does it all." They begin to see clearly that his grace is so far out of proportion to their measly little efforts that it's downright humbling. What can they do but say "Thank you, thank you, thank you," and go on with the daily practice. It might be quite apparent to them that if any spiritual progress is going to happen, it will all be due to grace.

And they're right.

Two different ways of experiencing the truth of 'He does it all'. One is a trap, the other the pathway to dissolving the ego and ultimately experiencing grace.

ILLUSION: A perfect living master should . . .

When we assume we know how a perfect living master should dress, how he should look, how he should speak, move, gesticulate and behave, we should pause and reflect for a moment – what on earth are we doing?

Aren't we bringing assumptions from our own cultural traditions and prejudices and trying to use them as a yardstick to measure the living master? Really? Just stop and think a moment. Obviously we know that if we come from a Chinese background, we will have one set of expectations; if our background is European, we will have different expectations. If we come from a Sikh background, we will have expectations specific to that tradition. And if our family members have been initiates of the masters of the Radha Soami lineage in Beas, we have our expectations too.

What if the master behaves differently from our expectations? Do we then get shaken? Do we find ourselves doubting whether he's a perfect master after all because he doesn't conform to our idea of the perfect master?

What if the master were to appoint as his successor someone from a different country, a different culture, someone who had never worn a turban in his or her life? What if he were to appoint a woman? Would we accept the new master or decide the successor could not be a true master and give up on the path?

The delusion that we know what a perfect master should be like could derive from the word 'perfect'. The Indian term *'puran sant satguru'* is generally translated into English as 'perfect master'. The literal meaning of *'puran'* is complete, nothing lacking. He is a *'complete'* master because his realization is complete instead of partial.

The word 'perfect' might give us the idea that the master should never get sick, or should not have a mark on his face, or should never mispronounce a word. Do we think the idea that he is 'perfect' means that he should not joke and laugh, or should not sing and dance at a wedding, wear jeans or eat ice cream? These characteristics relate to external realities and not to the spiritual reality of the living master.

The present master has explained that the English-language word 'perfect' or 'perfection' can imply going to extremes. He has pointed out that being 'complete' means that the master is balanced. He is fully, completely balanced.

There is a grave danger – a real trap – in thinking we know how a perfect master should look or act. Once someone asked Maharaj Charan Singh to comment on why Great Master had done or said a particular thing. His response was: "That, he knows best. We are too low to judge these things. He knows best. You see, only they know how these birds fly who can fly along with the birds. While sitting on the ground we cannot know or appreciate the flying of the birds."

A living master – a *puran sant satguru* – can probably be counted on to do one thing: that is to surprise us. If we have preconceived ideas about how a master should look and act, the master will probably confuse us by looking and acting differently, and changing the way things are done.

Just as there is a danger of getting attached to concepts, there is a particular danger in attaching too much importance to the outward appearance of the physical form of the master. The master's appearance will change, as all things in the physical world change. The physical form of the master is, after all . . . physical. If he gets sick, it can even shake our faith in the path. After all, no one looks their best when they're sick.

Master Wang, a Taoist master of the sixteenth century, had a large number of disciples. In fact, more and more disciples were flocking to him, and he knew that many of them were not sincere. So he deliberately caused his appearance to change. Boils erupted all over his body, and he got so weak and frail he could hardly stand or walk. Many of his so-called disciples were horrified. They believed that a true master would be above getting sick. He should control his body and the forces of nature to his personal advantage – and that would mean that outwardly he would remain 'perfect'. So they went away in disgust. Once they had left and Master Wang saw that only the real disciples were still there, the ones he wanted to pass his true teaching on to, his mysterious sickness ended and he resumed teaching.

Our preconceived notions about what the master is, or should be, are based on a lifetime of cultural programming and layers of misconceptions and illusions. Let us approach the challenge of being disciples of a perfect master with open minds – as clean slates – and allow the master to reveal himself to us, to show his real self, one facet at a time.

LET'S GET REAL

The power to turn Sant Mat
into merely a social organization
is not in the hands of the organization.
It is not even a decision made —
consciously or unconsciously —
by the collective action of the sangat.
It is a choice we each make
every day when we decide
whether or not we will meditate
as instructed at our initiation.
The question is not 'out there'
but very much 'in here'.
It is our decision,
a decision for each one of us.

Let's go beyond comforting concepts

Let's wake from these dreams and illusions

Let's experience Truth in all its simplicity

Let's get real

12

THE MYSTERY
OF THE LIVING MASTER

How do we go beyond concepts? Meditation is the method, but the guidance of a living master is a vital ingredient in that method. As the Sufi master Al-Qushayri put it: "Each wayfarer needs a master from whom he can learn his path, one breath at a time."

To learn our path one breath at a time means learning it moment by moment. From the living example of the living master we learn something that can't be put in words. Moment by moment, we learn our path in the atmosphere of the true master's presence. And most vitally, we learn our path through implicitly obeying our master's instructions, trusting him and following where he leads.

As any disciple can attest, it is the living guide that breathes life into the spiritual path. Without the living presence of a guide we can spend our lives going round and round in circles. If we want to become more conscious, awake, alive, we have to imbibe these qualities from one who is conscious, awake, alive.

Soami Ji points out that all the creation can be divided into that which is *chaitanya* (alive, alert, awake, conscious) and that which is *jarr* (inert, dead, unconscious). Then he states bluntly, "All except the Sat Guru come under the classification of *jarr* (inert). Only the Sat Guru is *chaitanya* (awakened) in this world."

It is the true master alone who can give humanity its true wake-up call.

Our beloved master – who is he?

Is the master God?

The present master has responded to this question: How can the unlimited be the limited?

Yet we read the words of Great Master: "The body of a master walks on this earth, but his soul soars to the seven skies. He is human in outer form, but God speaks through him. He is in reality God. He is God plus man, that is, a God-man. He is the string that connects us with God. The master is the Shabd personified, but he has to take a human form so that he may make us understand him."

The present master – the master of our own times – em-phasizes that the true guru is the Shabd. The physical body of the master is short-lived and finite. How, the present master asks, can that be 'God'? Can God be limited to, defined by and imprisoned within a human body?

The real master-disciple relationship, he stresses, is on the inside. This is his constant emphasis. The Shabd is the real master, and we become a real disciple when our attention is attuned to the Shabd within.

Yet we are fond of quoting the many poems and hymns by saints in the Bhakti tradition, as well as the letters and satsangs from masters in the Radha Soami lineage, saying the master is God. We even delight in the perplexing statement that the master is greater than God! We are thrilled, inspired and awestruck by such statements.

This must be the greatest paradox of all paradoxes for any disciple.

The present master explains that the sole purpose of the physical outer master is to guide us to the real master on the inside, the Shabd.

From our limited perspective, we go on struggling to understand. We want clear answers: Is he God, or isn't he? When we see him during darshan or hear him giving satsang, are we seeing and hearing a mere human being?

The present master says emphatically that there is nothing 'mere' about being human. He says we all have the 'God particle' in us. That is our unique privilege as human beings. We all have the potential to realize God. He says that spirituality is given to all of us in equal measure. It's just a matter of realization. When asked if he could describe himself in a single word, he said: Sevadar.

Can we draw benefit from the present master's emphasis?

We like the concept that the master is God, yet we do have to recognize that it is a concept, a rough approximation of a reality we are not yet equipped to understand. The fact is that we don't have a clue who or what God is. So, until we have a direct experience of the divine, what difference will it make to the practice we have committed to do, if we claim the master is, or is not, God?

"The master is God" is a concept. "The master is not God" is a concept. "The master is sort of God and sort of not God" is a concept.

We have to go beyond concepts.

The relationship of God to the master is, for us, a mystery. Do we want to know the nature of the master? We will have to go to a higher level of consciousness. Do we want to know the nature of God? We will have to go to a higher level. There is no alternative. Clinging to a concept and making it an article of faith will not help. Hanging on with a tight grip to an illusion will never help us to grow spiritually.

We have no choice. There is only one way. The present master often tells us that our parameters are too narrow; we need to open our parameters wider. From our narrow, confined perspective on life, we need to see the bigger picture. So we have to take the steps that will reveal the reality.

Trust

The spiritual reality the master points us toward may be beyond our experience, and therefore just a set of concepts for us. We do, however, have some experience of the master. We know something about what we feel in his presence, some-thing about the atmosphere that surrounds him. We may have heard him give satsang, or answer questions, or even make jokes. We may have seen him as he bows deeply, then takes his seat to give satsang. Experiences are not concepts.

For some of us the first experience of seeing or hearing the master may have struck us with an immediate recognition – love at first sight, taking us by surprise. Falling in love – most people have that experience sometime in their lives. Out of that relationship come immediate faith, confidence and trust.

Others may have come slowly and gradually to trust and to ask for initiation, after years of considering the teachings and wondering whether this was the right teacher and the right path for them.

In either case, it probably takes years of practice on the spiritual path before we can go from a superficial acceptance of the master and his teaching to an unquestioning, unshake-able trust borne of deepening love.

A warrior and his wife were crossing over to an island on a small boat. Suddenly a fierce storm rocked their little boat. Tossed wildly about, with waves crashing over the sides, the boat seemed about to capsize. The wife was terrified, know-ing that if the boat went down they would surely drown. She started trembling and crying. Meanwhile, the warrior sat motionless. The wife pleaded with her husband to do some-thing to save them. He just continued to sit there without moving, as if he were totally at peace.

Over the noise of the storm she called out to him, "Are you just going to let us drown? Why don't you do something?"

The warrior silently pulled his sword out of its sheath and held it menacingly against her throat. She started laughing.

"Why are you laughing?" he asked. "This sword is razor sharp. Just one movement and it'll slit your throat."

To which she confidently replied, "The sword might be dangerous, but it is in your hands. And that is enough for me. I trust you completely, that's why I'm not afraid."

The warrior put the sword back in its sheath saying, "Just so, this storm is in my master's hands, that's why I'm not afraid."

———

We too are trying to cross storm-tossed waters to the distant shore of Truth. So long as we trust our own intellect to understand the spiritual path, the mind will be in turmoil, churning, trying to make sense of things. If we trust the master, we will put his instructions into action.

Dancing on the edge of a sword

In spirituality, true learning begins when the mind drops its objections, love and trust take charge, the mind becomes still, and we enter a deep silence. We become receptive. We become open. We finally are ready for learning beyond what we think we know. When the mind surrenders to silence there are no waves rippling the surface, no preconceptions, no wavering. There is only calmness, serenity and alertness.

It doesn't take intellect to understand Truth. It doesn't take study of the scriptures. It doesn't take analysis to grasp the truths the master teaches. Often an unlettered person will understand, while a highly learned scholar misses the point. It takes love. It takes trust. It takes openness and attentiveness. It takes absence of ego and relaxed receptivity.

The present master often relates the story of a wise man who was invited to speak to a group of students. He arrived and asked the assembled students whether they knew what he was going to talk about. They all said, "Yes." And the wise man said, "Well, if you already know what I'm going to talk about then there's no point in my saying it." And he left.

The students again invited him to speak. Before starting his talk he asked, "Do you know what I'm going to talk about?" They all said, "No." And he responded, "If you don't know what I'm going to talk about, then why am I here?" And he left.

The students invited him to speak yet again. This time when he asked whether they knew what he was going to talk about, they were prepared. Half of them said, "Yes," and half of them said, "No." The wise man said, "Then those who know can explain it to those who don't know, and there's no point in my staying here." And he left.

One more time the students invited the wise man to speak to them. This time when he asked whether they knew what he was going to talk about they were all silent. This was the moment he was waiting for, and he stayed and began to share his teachings with them.

At our level of understanding, we can only conclude that the master is a mystery. Even if we don't understand everything, we can be obedient to his instructions. We can carry on trying to follow him in trust and obedience along a pathway that may seem to us like a thin, sharp edge between contradictory perspectives.

Discipleship is not tea at Auntie's, as Kabir, the medieval Indian mystic, said. Discipleship on the mystical path has been described as a dance with our Lord, our Beloved, on the edge of a sword. It has been said that once you come out to dance, there is no question of feeling shy.

Infinite in his freedom

Jewish spiritual masters have been described as infinite or outstanding in their freedom, an expression that can easily be applied to perfect masters of all times. The master is infinitely free to traverse the higher realms of creation. He is infinitely free to live in the lower and intermediary worlds. He is infinitely free to interpret scripture according to his own experience. He is infinitely free in how he gives his teachings. He is infinitely free in how he reaches the people and gets through to them. He may give discourses, sing, recite poems, dance, make jokes or remain silent.

If we think we can predict what a master will do or say, we are mistaken. We are limited; we do not yet have access to his world of oneness. If we think a master should be serious he will joke and tease. If we think a master should follow the traditions of the past he will break with tradition. A master is not caged in the confines of our ways of thinking. He is not programmed. He is free. Infinitely free.

And full of surprises!

Sometimes a master may wake us up by deliberately behaving in ways that shock us. There is a story of a master who was walking through the marketplace with a group of his disciples. A pretty girl walked by, and the master said, "Oh! The Lord is beautiful!" and kissed the girl. Each of the disciples copied him, reverently repeating, "Oh! The Lord is beautiful!" as they kissed the girl.

Next they passed a blacksmith shop, where the blacksmith was hammering a glowing, red-hot piece of iron on the anvil. The master cried out, "Oh! The Lord is beautiful!" and kissed the red-hot iron.

None of the disciples followed suit.

Though they held back, they did not miss the lesson in the master's strange actions. Everything is the Lord's, and the Lord pervades everything. His beauty shines forth in everything.

Without the living guidance of a master, seekers would remain stuck in philosophical speculation. We could spend our whole lives in metaphysical discussions, or engaged in ascetic practices that punish the body but leave the mind untouched. Even the most ardent seeker after Truth would go round and round in a circle defined by the limitations of his own perspective and experience. But if we follow a living master – put our trust in him, act on his instructions, and follow him where he leads – we can break free.

The highest seva
is meditation

13

A WAY OF LIFE TO BE LIVED

The masters teach us a way of living, a way of approaching our lives, which can turn all our time and all our actions into 'meditation'. If we attend to the meditation practice each day and then live a true Sant Mat way of life, we live in the atmosphere of meditation all day. As Maharaj Charan Singh said: "If you build that atmosphere of meditation and you live in that atmosphere . . . then every breath is meditation."

Sant Mat has been called a school of practical mysticism. It is practical because it is to be practised; and practical because it relates to every down-to-earth aspect of our daily lives. As Maharaj Charan Singh put it: "Sant Mat is an attitude of mind to be developed and a way of life to be lived." Rather than thinking about Truth, or discussing and analysing concepts about Truth, we try to live it here and now, in the way we conduct our daily lives.

> Live in the atmosphere of meditation and every breath is meditation

The present master was once asked, What is the minimum amount of time we need to spend in meditation each day? He gave a startling answer: Twenty-four hours.

Living in obedience and surrender

How do we live a way of life where everything becomes meditation? The life of a disciple, a novice and learner, begins with obedience, plain and simple. Without obedience to our master's instructions, we may as well not have asked for initiation. In the memorable words of Soami Ji, implicit obedience to the master of our time is "the long and short of everything".

The first step in obedience is to obey the simple directive to attend to meditation every day without regard to whether we feel like it or not, whether we achieve results or not, and whether other demands on our time crop up or not. Obedience means: just do it. Just do our meditation. Give our time daily to the meditation practice he has asked us to do. As Great Master used to ask of his disciples when they met: "Have you done my work?"

The implicit obedience Soami Ji described – obedience that leaves no room for the intervention of one's own cleverness or objections – is the beginning of a life of surrender. While true surrender is a lofty ideal, and we may think of it as something we will attain at some distant time in the future, this simple act of showing up for meditation practice each day is a big step in the direction of that lofty goal.

We can carry this same attitude of implicit obedience into all the activities of our lives, and it will lead to a relaxed, happy and peaceful life. The masters guide us to make the words of the master the rule of our life. His words and his guidance then form a foundation on which we build a worry-free life.

This one action – implicitly following our master's guidance without allowing our own reasoning to object – covers so much. It leads us to forgive where we'd rather hold a grudge, to be kind and compassionate where we'd rather be selfish, to be content where we'd rather grumble and complain.

The consequence and enormity of surrender to a saint can make a sinner into a saint. Remaining in obedience can keep us in the carefree bliss of discipleship forever. Just consider how all of the masters have remained disciples throughout their lives. Consider how each master has said his master is in charge of everything. It is he who is doing everything. The master sees himself only as a sevadar, doing the task his master has asked him to do.

It has been said that surrender is the most difficult thing in the world when you are doing it; but it is the easiest when it is done. Surrender is a state of an unquestioning mind coupled with implicit trust. However, it is important to remember that surrender is not demanded by a master; surrender can only be freely given.

Living gracefully and cheerfully

How can we live in the Lord's will? From a practical point of view, for all of us who have no ability to discern the will of God, all we can do is to accept and deal cheerfully with whatever situations arise in our lives. We can believe that whatever situations we face, these have been allotted to us because they are for our best and highest good.

'Highest good' may include undergoing pain and pruning. Pain is a part of growth. We are undergoing and clearing our karma. So whatever circumstances we find ourselves in, whatever the challenges, whatever the hardships, or whatever the joys, we can believe they have all come to us according to the Lord's will. We make our best efforts to improve our lot, but we accept however it works out as the Lord's will.

As wise elders – whether mystics or not – have always counselled: Do your best, and leave the rest. Leave the rest for the Lord to work out according to his will. Right action and surrender are two sides of one coin.

Doing our best is all we can do, because ultimately there is only His will.

"May the Will of Allah be done," a pious man said.
"It always is, in any case," said Mullah Nasruddin.
"How can you prove that, Mullah?" asked the man.
"Quite simply, if it wasn't always being done by His will, then surely at some time or another my will would be done, wouldn't it?"

As Mullah Nasruddin points out, no matter how much we want this or that to happen, in the end it is the Lord's will that prevails in life, not ours. The challenge is for us to accept this with good spirit. The present master once summed up a long and complicated question and answer exchange with one simple phrase: His will or nothing.

What is the impact of adopting this approach to life? We go through our karmas with equanimity. Rather than resisting, we accept and adjust to the ups and downs as they come. As Maharaj Charan Singh used to put it, we go through our karmas "gracefully and cheerfully".

Resisting the force of destiny shakes up our equilibrium, whereas acceptance brings equanimity within us. When we try to impose our will on existence, we invite disappointment. Wisdom – what to say of happiness and peace of mind – lies in adhering to the principle of 'His will or nothing'.

Going gracefully and cheerfully through our karmas, seeing them as the will of the Lord, gives us a positive attitude. This attitude carries us through the ups and downs of life without forgetting that our highest priority each day is meditation.

'His will or nothing.' As layers of meaning unfold, we discover that here is the core of spiritual life.

Keeping a balance

The master so often responds to questions with: Keep a balance. The questioner may not even have realized that he or she was going to extremes. Gradually, perhaps over a period of years as our understanding deepens, we come to see how profound his words are. Taking to heart the master's simple, down-to-earth advice can keep our lives on track.

'Keep a balance.' These three little words, said to us so often by the master of our time, are loaded with meaning and applicable to countless situations in our lives.

We get out of balance in so many ways: focusing on our jobs to the detriment of our families, obsessing over our children's lives and forgetting to take care of our own health, or staying up so late watching TV show after TV show that we fail to get up fresh and refreshed for meditation. If we get out of balance, we won't be able to sustain ourselves on our chosen path. So the master says: Keep a balance. In these simple words he compresses a multitude of actions, words and thoughts and gives us a deep reservoir of potential wisdom to draw upon.

Some may think that, since meditation is the key to the spiritual path, perhaps it would be best to spend as many hours each day in meditation as possible. We may think it best to avoid marriage, leave off developing any profession, not have children, live in solitude meditating all day. But senses that are then suppressed may become more sensitive; suppressed desires may become stronger. When we go to extremes, our God-given natural system begins to revolt; therefore we need to maintain a balance.

Therefore, the master says, live your life in the world; live the life of a householder. Spirituality can be practised by an ordinary householder. Masters also have families, yet they keep their balance.

A pendulum swings. The farther it swings in one direction, the farther it swings in the other. In that still point in the middle of the pendulum's arc we rest in the master's refuge. Even in the midst of the intense activity of a challenging life, with professional and family obligations, we can place ourselves in the master's refuge, and remain safe.

The secret is in keeping our balance.

Taking refuge

For most of us, learning to be a true disciple is a slow process – long and gradual, with whatever transformation it is making in us often being imperceptible to us. Slow and steady wins the race. It has been said that the path is more long than hard. Maharaj Charan Singh often said that this is the simplest of paths, but it is difficult to follow.

To sustain ourselves though the long years of practice, we need help. We need the support and protection of the master's refuge. Satsang and seva offer us a place where the atmosphere of the master's presence uplifts our spirits and bolsters our determination to be steadfast on the path.

The master's refuge keeps us safe from the assaults of a wayward mind; it draws us again and again back to the focus. We get muddled, and it reawakens clarity. Again and again, the master's refuge brings to our awareness the simplicity of the spiritual path. We remember and recommit to the real purpose of our lives.

The master's refuge is not a structure built with bricks and mortar, nor with wood or plaster or steel. There is only one material used in its construction and that is love. And there are only two people in the refuge – the master and the disciple. And his love embraces the whole.

Loving him

It is said that when bees are caught out in a storm, they hold fast to little stones to preserve their balance and keep from being blown away.

Like the bees, we can hold fast to our love for the master and preserve our balance through the storms of life. And if our love for the master seems weak or non-existent to us, we can be held fast by *his* love for *us* – which, as we go forward on this path, we will find is as wide as the whole world. His love for us is love for the Lord – for the All, for the One. He embraces all in his love. And in his eyes we too are part of that One, each of us.

We live through countless fleeting relationships, seeking, finding and losing. If we do not know it yet, then life teaches us that to expect perfect love in human relationships is a folly. Human life is perishable and short-lived. The love that holds us together, the one that is permanent, the one that encompasses our entire being, is the love between master and disciple, because at its depth it is the love between the Lord and the soul.

Our capacity to love is limited. The love the saints lead us to is not a matter of fluctuating emotions. The affection and gratitude we feel may be only a dim reflection of the real love, the love that dissolves all separations and leads to union.

How do we grow in this love? The master has given a simple answer. He says: Love means to give, give and give.

Give in totality, give completely and give entirely! No barriers. We are to just give wholeheartedly; give to a point of removing the self. No expectations, just giving. That is discipleship.

So we begin by giving the only gift we have to give – our time and attention. Two and a half hours of our time, accompanied by whatever amount of our attention we are able to gather and give. It is a small gift. It may seem to us a paltry gift when we consider the scattered attention we bring to the meditation practice. But nonetheless, it is a gift of love.

> **Love means to give**
> **and give and give**

14
THE MYSTIC PATH

The present master often ends his satsang with the following message to the sangat. He says: If you want to please your master, don't give lip service. With words, you'll get only words. With actions, you'll get results. Reflect your choice for spirituality through your actions. Make meditation your priority. If you give full time to your meditation practice, the Lord takes care of everything.

In other words: Walk the talk.

To every question the present master's answer is the same. To every problem the present master's solution is the same. Whether we ask for joy, grace, forgiveness or relief from pain, there is a firm one-word answer from him – very simply expressed: Meditation.

We may wonder, how can this one single answer be the solution to all problems? What about *my* very specific and unique problem? Will the answer always be meditation?

We are making a choice

The first step of the mystic path is forming the habit of meditation every single day.

To go in the direction we are seeking, perseverance is necessary. And that means sitting in meditation every day. As Maharaj Charan Singh put it: "Regularity in meditation gives confidence and strength that is difficult to acquire in any other way."

When the alarm goes off in the morning – in that one moment we make our choice. We can be up at the sound of the alarm, or we can turn off the alarm and go back to sleep. That one second shows what our priorities are. It shows whether we have understood the nature and the magnitude of the gift we have been given.

Just consider: What do we do when we're about to leave on a nice vacation? Say we have an early morning flight to catch. We might not even need to set the alarm. We'd probably stay up all night too excited to sleep. We'd be humming and smiling and bouncy on our feet. Our bags would be packed and we'd be raring to go! And this is just a vacation; it will end in a week or two and then put us back in the 'same old grind'.

———

Mullah Nasruddin didn't go to the office one day. In the evening he told his friend he was very happy because he had slept all day. His friend asked if he had taken leave from work.

Mullah Nasruddin replied, "No, but I tossed a coin in the morning to see whether I had to go to work or not – if it came down heads, I'd have to go to work; if it was tails, I could take the day off."

"So it came down tails?" he was asked.

"Yes," he replied, "but I had to toss it ten times before it came to tails."

Is our approach to meditation like Mullah Nasruddin's to his job?

Habits are a powerful force. We all know how to create a new habit: just do the same thing over and over, day after day, and soon we can't help doing that thing. Force of habit pushes us to do it. We can choose to make full use of this powerful force.

> Regularity in meditation gives confidence and strength

The proverb, "As the twig is bent, so the tree is inclined," holds true here. We can decide this very day to establish the direction and the habits that will carry us through the years. We can choose to let the force of habit work for us, not against us.

Meditation

The power of daily meditation is inexpressible. The present master expressed the potential of even our feeblest of efforts at meditation when he said to a young initiate during a question and answer session: Just make one mark and I'll add the zeros.

The confused young fellow said, Huh? So the master explained: You put the one, and I'll add two zeros, so it's a hundred. One hundred per cent!

Then he added: But it has to start with you.

When we think of it in this way, it surely would have to start with us. If a master were to put two zeros or even a hundred zeros, without that single mark we make on the paper – our little 'one' – it still would remain zero. But with our one and his two zeros, it's one hundred! One hundred per cent!

If an investment bank ever offered such a deal, we'd jump at it. Imagine the advertisement: invest one dollar and we'll make it a hundred. And if we put in one dollar every day, we'd soon be rolling in wealth.

By repeatedly insisting on meditation for every situation or problem, the master drives home the fact that daily meditation is a process. It is a gradual process that slowly detaches us from the physical and attaches us to the spiritual. This process helps us in dealing with the everyday pains of life without getting affected, without letting situations get under our skin. The practice of meditation works as a shock absorber during turbulent times. The awareness we get through meditation brings equanimity within us and generates inner strength.

Meditation is our responsibility; it has to be an individual's effort. No one else can do it for us. No one else can make us sit for meditation practice. We have to choose to do it. It is a choice we make freely, out of love.

A disciple once asked his master, "Can you say something about God?"

The master replied, "Meditate."

The disciple was astonished. "Just that, one word?"

The master again said, "Meditate."

The disciple was puzzled. "You keep repeating yourself," he said.

The master again said, "Meditate. Nothing more can be said about it. You have to do it. You will have to do it."

No one can talk about God. God is beyond all words. But God can be known. Meditate. As it says in the Bible: "Be still and know that I am God."

So we just have to do it. The one and only directive: Do the meditation!

Getting real

We often say that Sant Mat is a path of 'self-realization' and 'God-realization'. What is 'realization'? What does it mean to 'realize' something?

In ordinary usage, 'realization' means something is already a fact, already true, already present – only we weren't aware. We didn't *real*-ize it. For us it was not *real*. For example, suppose we're very focused on some task – cooking, reading, balancing the bank statement – and our friend walks into the room. We don't notice, so our friend waits. Then we look around, surprised, and say, "Oh! I didn't realize you were there!"

Sant Mat is a path of realization in this same sense. It is a way of waking up to life's most profound reality. Our friend – our real friend – is standing right here by our side and we don't realize it.

The present master explains that we are supported by Shabd all the time. We just don't realize it. Master gives us the wake-up call. Every moment we are cared for by Shabd, all of us. We are under the protection of Shabd. We are sustained by Shabd. We are enlivened by Shabd. Shabd is what we are. Right now. Without Shabd we wouldn't be alive; we wouldn't exist. Actually . . . we *are* Shabd.

Our spiritual 'journey' is simply a matter of waking up to this fact. We are not really traversing a journey to a distant goal, though we often use that metaphor. We are only realizing what is already true. Right here. Right now. Within us. About us. For us.

Meditation is the technique by which we wake up to what is real. From the uncontrolled and scattered thought flow that now clouds and confuses our perception of reality, we come gradually to a place of clarity and stillness. We realize who and what we are.

Our companion – our dear and trusted master – is our friend throughout this process. First we know him as the human being who sits on the dais, the human being who instructs us and answers our questions – a human being who has particular mannerisms, dress sense, modes of expression, a human being who lives in a particular place, perhaps far from where we live.

Gradually, through the meditation process, we will come to know him as a presence. We will become aware of his presence in our life, especially, and more clearly, his presence in our meditation. The idea that he is within us, waiting for us at the eye centre, slowly and slowly becomes real to us. Not a mere idea, not a concept or a teaching, but an experience. We, who have been lonely for so long, discover that we are not alone, have never been alone – that he is always with us, loving us. We have never been separated from him.

With proper practice, with regularity and application, the disciple eventually comes to know that master and Shabd are one. It is then that the statement repeated so often in satsang – that the real guru is the Shabd and the real disciple is the attention attuned to Shabd's divine melody – becomes real.

When through his grace we begin to hear the Shabd ringing within us, we wake up to the reality that was always there. The mystics tell us that this experience is beyond the greatest joy the mind can imagine and beyond the highest knowledge the intellect can ever acquire. The infinite magnitude of that experience is beyond human comprehension. This is the Truth we seek.

Let's enjoy the reality that is all around us and within us. Let us be mindful to reflect its splendour in all we do. Let's wake up.

Spirituality –
Caught Not Taught

LAST WORDS

Let's circle back to the opening question of our book: What is our objective?

Do we want concepts and illusions? Do we want words? Or do we want to awaken to spirituality and experience a truth that never dies?

We came to a living master and asked for initiation for a reason. The masters enable us to see a new way of life, one where we know we are spiritual beings, just going right now through physical and mental experiences. We belong to a realm of oneness that exists eternally beyond the limitations of words and concepts. We belong to a world that is true forever.

As initiates we decide what we want every day. It is the choice we make every day, a choice that is ours alone. It does not lie in the hands of any organization, any other person, any other power or circumstance. It's a decision we make ourselves.

This choice we make when we decide whether or not we will give our time and attention to our meditation practice as our master has instructed us.

GLOSSARY

Adi Granth   the scripture comprising the hymns of the Sikh Gurus and numerous saints of the Indian subcontinent.

bhajan   the practice of listening to the creative sound current in meditation.

bhakti   the practice of devotion; used also to describe the Indian mystic tradition of self- and God-realization through cultivating devotion.

causal plane   the most refined of the three planes of existence (physical, astral and causal) below the realm of pure spirit.

Charan Singh Maharaj   the master at Beas from 1951 to 1990.

darshan   vision or sight of the master done with deep respect, devotion and attention.

Dera   Dera Baba Jaimal Singh, the headquarters of the Radha Soami Satsang Beas society in India.

Great Master   an affectionate term used to refer to Sawan Singh Ji Maharaj, the master at Beas from 1902 to 1948.

Hazur   a term of respect for Maharaj Charan Singh, the master at Beas from 1951 to 1990.

karma   action and reaction; the law of cause and effect; the fruits of past actions.

langar   the free kitchen of the guru's community.

Nam   Name (*naam*); the divine energy that creates and sustains the universe; term used interchangeably with Shabd.

pandal   used here to refer to the open-sided shed where large satsangs are held.

parshad   a blessing; generally used to refer to blessed food.

Radiant Form   the inner, Shabd or light form of the master that one may see on entering the inner planes.

sangat   community of disciples.

Sant Mat   the teachings or path (*mat*) of the saints (*sant*).

Sardar Bahadur   a term of respect for Jagat Singh Maharaj, the master at Beas from 1948 to 1951.

Sat Guru   also written *satguru* as a single word, means literally the true guru, and is used as a term to designate the enlightened teacher living on earth.

satsang   the company (*sang*) of Truth (*sat*); a gathering of devotees where a spiritual discourse is given.

satsang ghar   used here to refer to the large satsang hall at Dera, Beas, built under the supervision of Maharaj Sawan Singh in the 1930s.

satsangi   in common usage, one who has been initiated by a spiritual master; esoterically, one who has come into the company of Truth, Shabd, Nam.

Sawan Singh Maharaj   the master at Beas from 1902 to 1948.

seva   selfless service.

Shabd   Sound, Word; the current of divine energy that creates and sustains the universe.

simran   the practice of silent repetition of a mantra to still the mind.

sinchit karma   the stored fruits of past actions from which destiny for each lifetime is shaped.

Soami Ji Maharaj   a term of respect for Seth Shiv Dayal Singh of Agra, who taught the path of Shabd from 1861 to 1878.

BOOKS ON THIS SCIENCE

RSSB TRADITION

Sar Bachan Prose – *Soami Ji Maharaj*
Sar Bachan Poetry – *Soami Ji Maharaj*
Spiritual Letters – *Baba Jaimal Singh*

The Dawn of Light – *Maharaj Sawan Singh*
Discourses on Sant Mat, Volume I – *Maharaj Sawan Singh*
My Submission – *Maharaj Sawan Singh*
Philosophy of the Masters (5 volumes) – *Maharaj Sawan Singh*
Spiritual Gems – *Maharaj Sawan Singh*

Discourses on Sant Mat, Volume II – *Maharaj Jagat Singh*
The Science of the Soul – *Maharaj Jagat Singh*

Die to Live – *Maharaj Charan Singh*
Divine Light – *Maharaj Charan Singh*
Light on Saint John – *Maharaj Charan Singh*
Light on Saint Matthew – *Maharaj Charan Singh*
Light on Sant Mat – *Maharaj Charan Singh*
The Path – *Maharaj Charan Singh*
Quest for Light – *Maharaj Charan Singh*
Spiritual Discourses (2 volumes) – *Maharaj Charan Singh*
Spiritual Heritage – *Maharaj Charan Singh*
Spiritual Perspectives (3 volumes) – *Maharaj Charan Singh*

Call of the Great Master – *Daryai Lal Kapur*
Concepts & Illusions: A Perspective – *Sabina Oberoi*
Heaven on Earth – *Daryai Lal Kapur*
Honest Living – *M. F. Singh*
In Search of the Way – *Flora E. Wood*
The Inner Voice – *C. W. Sanders*
Liberation of the Soul – *J. Stanley White*
Life Is Fair: The Law of Cause and Effect – *Brian Hines*
Living Meditation – *Hector Esponda Dubin*
Message Divine – *Shanti Sethi*
The Mystic Philosophy of Sant Mat – *Peter Fripp*
Mysticism: The Spiritual Path – *Lekh Raj Puri*
The Path of the Masters – *Julian P. Johnson*
Radha Soami Teachings – *Lekh Raj Puri*
A Soul's Safari – *Netta Pfeifer*
A Spiritual Primer – *Hector Esponda Dubin*
Treasure beyond Measure – *Shanti Sethi*
A Wake Up Call: Beyond Concepts & Illusions –
 Sabina Oberoi and Beverly Chapman
With a Great Master in India – *Julian P. Johnson*
With the Three Masters (3 volumes) – *Rai Sahib Munshi Ram*

MYSTIC TRADITION

Bulleh Shah – *J. R. Puri and T. R. Shangari*
Dadu: The Compassionate Mystic – *K. N. Upadhyaya*
Dariya Sahib: Saint of Bihar – *K. N. Upadhyaya*
Guru Nanak: His Mystic Teachings – *J. R. Puri*
Guru Ravidas: The Philosopher's Stone – *K. N. Upadhyaya*
Kabir: The Great Mystic – *Isaac A. Ezekiel*
Kabir: The Weaver of God's Name – *V. K. Sethi*

Many Voices, One Song: The Poet Mystics of Maharashtra –
Judith Sankaranarayan
Mira: The Divine Lover – *V. K. Sethi*
Saint Namdev – *J. R. Puri and V. K. Sethi*
Sant Charandas – *T. R. Shangari*
Sant Paltu: His Life and Teachings – *Isaac A. Ezekiel*
Sarmad: Martyr to Love Divine – *Isaac A. Ezekiel*
Shams-e Tabrizi – *Farida Maleki*
Sheikh Farid: The Great Sufi Mystic – *T. R. Shangari*
Sultan Bahu – *J. R. Puri and K. S. Khak*
The Teachings of Goswami Tulsidas – *K. N. Upadhyaya*
Tukaram: The Ceaseless Song of Devotion – *C. Rajwade*
Tulsi Sahib: Saint of Hathras – *J. R. Puri and V. K. Sethi*
Voice of the Heart: Songs of Devotion from the Mystics

MYSTICISM IN WORLD RELIGIONS
Adventure of Faith – *Shraddha Liertz*
Buddhism: Path to Nirvana – *K. N. Upadhyaya*
The Divine Romance – *John Davidson*
The Gospel of Jesus – *John Davidson*
Gurbani Selections (Volumes I, II)
The Holy Name: Mysticism in Judaism – *Miriam Caravella*
Jap Ji – *T. R. Shangari*
The Mystic Heart of Judaism – *Miriam Caravella*
The Odes of Solomon – *John Davidson*
One Being One – *John Davidson*
Pathways to Liberation: Exploring the Vedic Tradition –
K. Sankaranarayanan
The Prodigal Soul – *John Davidson*
The Song of Songs – *John Davidson*
Tales of the Mystic East
A Treasury of Mystic Terms, Parts I–II (10 volumes) – *John Davidson, ed.*
Yoga and the Bible – *Joseph Leeming*

VEGETARIAN COOKBOOKS
Baking Without Eggs
British Taste
Creative Vegetarian Cooking
The Green Way to Healthy Living
Meals with Vegetables

BOOKS FOR CHILDREN
The Journey of the Soul – *Victoria Jones*
One Light Many Lamps – *Victoria Jones*

MISCELLANEOUS THEMES
Empower Women: An Awakening – *Leena Chawla*
Equilibrium of Love: Dera Baba Jaimal Singh

For Internet orders, please visit: www.rssb.org

For book orders within India, please write to:
Radha Soami Satsang Beas
BAV Distribution Centre, 5 Guru Ravi Dass Marg
Pusa Road, New Delhi 110 005

ADDRESSES FOR INFORMATION AND BOOKS

INDIAN SUBCONTINENT

INDIA
The Secretary
Radha Soami Satsang Beas
Dera Baba Jaimal Singh
District Amritsar
Punjab 143 204

NEPAL
Mr. S.B.B. Chhetri
RSSB - Kathmandu
Gongabu 7, P.O. Box 1646
Kathmandu
☎ +977-01-435-7765

SRI LANKA
Mrs. Maya Mahbubani
RSSB - Colombo
No. 47/1 Silva Lane
Rajagiriya, Colombo
☎ +94-11-286-1491

SOUTHEAST ASIA

Mrs. Cami Moss
RSSB - Hong Kong
T.S.T., P.O. Box 90745
Kowloon, Hong Kong
☎ +852-2369-0625

Mr. Manoj Sabnani
RSSB - Hong Kong
27th Floor, Tower B
Billion Centre
1 Wang Kwong Road
Kowloon Bay, Hong Kong
☎ +852-2369-0625

Mrs. Ivy Sabnani
Unit D, 22nd Floor, Tower A
Billion Center
1 Wang Kwong Road
Kowloon Bay, Hong Kong

HONG KONG
RSSB - Hong Kong
27th Floor, Tower B
Billion Centre
1 Wang Kwong Road
Kowloon Bay
☎ +852-2369-0625

GUAM
Mrs. Rekha Sadhwani
625 Alupang Cove
241 Condo Lane
Tamuning 96911

INDONESIA
Mr. Ramesh Sadarangani
Yayasan RSSB - Jakarta
Jl. Transyogi Kelurahan
Jatirangga
Pondok Gede 17434
☎ +62-21-845-1612

Yayasan RSSB - Bali
Jalan Bung Tomo
Desa Pemecutan Raya
Denpasar, Bali 80118
☎ +62-361-438-522

JAPAN
Mr. Jani G. Mohinani
RSSB - Kobe
1-2-18 Nakajima-Dori
Aotani, Chuo-Ku
Kobe 651-0052
☎ +81-78-222-5353

KOREA
Mr. Haresh Buxani
SOS Study Centre - Korea
638, Hopyeong-Dong
R603-1 & 604 Sungbo
Building
Nam Yangju, Gyeong Gi-Do
☎ +82-231-511-7008

MALAYSIA
Mr. Bhupinder Singh
RSSB - Kuala Lumpur
29 Jalan Cerapu Satu
Off Batu 3 ¼, Jalan Cheras
Kuala Lumpur 56100
Wilayah Persekutuan
☎ +603-9200-3073

PHILIPPINES
Mr. Anil Buxani
SOS Study Centre - Manila
9001 Don Jesus Boulevard
Alabang Hills, Cupang
Muntinlupa City, 1771
Metro Manila
☎ +63-2-772-0111 / 0555

SINGAPORE
Mrs. Asha Melwani
RSSB - Singapore
19 Amber Road
Singapore 439868
☎ +65-6447-4956

TAIWAN, R.O.C.
Mr. Haresh Buxani
SOS Study Centre - Taiwan
Aetna Tower Office
15F., No. 27-9, Sec.2
Jhongjheng E.Rd.
Danshuei Township
Taipei 25170
☎ +886-2-8809-5223

THAILAND
Mr. Harmahinder Singh Sethi
RSSB - Bangkok
58/32 Thaphra
Ratchadaphisek Road
Soi 16, Wat Thapra
Bangkok Yai District
Bangkok 10600
☎ +66-2-868-2186 / 2187

ASIA PACIFIC

AUSTRALIA
Mrs. Jill Wiley
P.O. Box 1256
Kenmore 4069, Queensland

SOS Study Centre - Sydney
1530 Elizabeth Drive
Cecil Park
New South Wales 2178
☎ +61-2-9826-2599

NEW ZEALAND
Mr. Tony Waddicor
P.O. Box 5331, Auckland

SOS Study Centre - Auckland
80 Olsen Avenue,
Hillsborough, Auckland
☎ +64-9-624-2202

CANADA & UNITED STATES

CANADA
Mr. John Pope
5285 Coombe Lane, Belcarra
British Columbia V3H 4N6

SOS Study Centre - Vancouver
2932 -176th Street
Surrey, B.C. V3S 9V4
☎ +1-604-541-4792

Mrs. Meena Khanna
149 Elton Park Road
Oakville, Ontario L6J 4C2

155

SOS Study Centre - Toronto
6566 Sixth Line, RR 1 Hornby
Ontario L0P 1E0
☎ +1-905-875-4579

UNITED STATES
Dr. Frank E. Vogel
275 Cutts Road
Newport, NH 03773

Dr. Douglas Graham Torr
529 Carolina Meadows Villa
Chapel Hill, NC 27517

Mr. Michael Sanderson
1104 Toppe Ridge Court
Raleigh, NC 27615

Mr. Gaurav Chawla
36689 Rolf St.
Westland, MI 48186

Mr. Hank Muller
P.O. Box 1847
Tomball, TX 77377

Mr. James Rosen
6710 Round Oak Road
Penngrove, CA 94951

Dr. Vincent P. Savarese
2550 Pequeno Circle
Palm Springs, CA 92264-9522

SOS Study Centre -
Fayetteville
4115 Gillespie Street
Fayetteville, NC 28306-9053
☎ +1-910-426-5306

SOS Study Centre - Petaluma
2415 Washington Street
Petaluma, CA 94954
☎ +1-707-762-5082

MEXICO & CENTRAL AMERICA

Dr. Servando Sanchez
16103 Vanderbilt Drive
Odessa, Florida 33556, USA

MEXICO
Mr. Francisco Rodriguez Rosas
RSSB - Puerto Vallarta
Circuito Universidad #779
Col. Ejido Las Juntas
Delegacion, El pitillal CP
48290 Puerto Vallarta, Jalisco
☎ +52-322-299-1954

Radha Soami Satsang Beas -
Guadalajara
Efrain Gonzalez Luna
2051 Col. Americana
Guadalajara, Jalisco 44090
☎ +52-333-615-4942

BELIZE
Mrs. Milan Bhindu
Hotchandani
4633 Seashore Drive
P.O. Box 830, Belize City

PANAMA
Mr. Ashok Tikamdas Dinani
P.O. Box 0302-01000, Colon

SOUTH AMERICA

ARGENTINA
Ms. Fabiana Shilton
Leiva 4363 Capital Federal
C.P. 1427 Buenos Aires

BRAZIL
Ms. Angela Beatriz
Rua Padre Caravalito 391
Sao Paulo 05427100

CHILE
Mr. Vijay Harjani
Pasaje Cuatro No. 3438
Sector Chipana, Iquique

Fundacion RSSB - Santiago
Av. Apoquindo 4775
Oficina 1503, Las Condes
Santiago
☎ +56-22-884-6816

COLOMBIA
Mrs. Emma Orozco
Asociacion Cultural
RSSB - Medellin
Calle 48 No. 78A-30
P.O. Box 0108, Medellin
☎ +574-234-5130

ECUADOR
Mr. Miguel Egas H.
RSSB - Quito
Calle Marquez de Varela
OE 3-68y Avda. America
P.O. Box 17-21-115, Quito
☎ +5932-2-555-988

PERU
Mr. Carlos Fitts
Asociacion Cultural
RSSB - Lima
Av. Pardo #231, 12th Floor
Miraflores, Lima 18
☎ +511-651-2030

VENEZUELA
Mrs. Helen Paquin
RSSB - Caracas
Av. Los Samanes con
Av. Los Naranjos Conj
Res. Florida 335
La Florida, Caracas 1012
☎ +58-212-731-2208

CARIBBEAN

Mr. Sean Finnigan
SOS Study Centre - St. Maarten
P.O. Box 978, Phillipsburg
St. Maarten, Dutch Caribbean

Mrs. Jaya Sabnani
1 Sunset Drive South
Fort George Heights
St. Michael BB111 02
Barbados, W.I.

BARBADOS, W.I.
Mr. Deepak Nebhani
SOS Study Centre - Barbados
No. 10, 5th Avenue, Belleville
St. Michael BB11114
☎ +1-246-427-4761

CURACAO
Mrs. Hema Chandiramani
SOS Study Centre - Curacao
Kaya Scvi di Milon 6-9
Santa Catharina
☎ +599-9-747-0226

ST. MAARTEN
Mr. Prakash Vishindas
Daryanani
SOS Study Centre - St. Maarten
203 Oyster Pond Road
St. Maarten, Dutch Caribbean
☎ +1-721-547-0066

GRENADA, W.I.
Mr. Ajay Mahbubani
P.O. Box 820, St. Georges

GUYANA
Mrs. Indu Lalwani
155, Garnette Street
Newtown Kitty, Georgetown

HAITI, W.I
Ms. Evelyn Liautaud Quine
SOS Study Centre-Haiti
84, Autoroute de Delmas
(angle Delmas 18-A)
Saint-Martin
HT6120, Port-au-Prince

JAMAICA, W.I.
Mrs. Shamni Khiani
37A Leader Drive
Montego Bay

ST. THOMAS
Mr. Rajesh Chatlani
5178 Dronningens Gade, Ste2
US Virgin Islands
VI 00801-6145

SURINAME
Mr. Ettire Stanley Rensch
Surinamestraat 36
Paramaribo

TRINIDAD, W.I.
Mr. Chandru Chatlani
20 Admiral Court
Westmoorings-by-Sea

EUROPE

BELGIUM
Mr. Piet J. E. Vosters
Driezenstraat 26
Turnhout 2300

BULGARIA
Mr. Deyan Stoyanov
Foundation RSSB - Bulgaria
P.O. Box 39, 8000 Bourgas

CYPRUS
Mr. Heraclis Achilleos
P.O. Box 29077
1035 Nicosia

CZECH REPUBLIC
Mr. Vladimir Skalsky
Maratkova 916
142 00 Praha 411

DENMARK
Mr. Tony Sharma
Sven Dalsgaardsvej 33
DK-7430 Ikast

SOS Study Centre - Denmark
Formervangen 36
Glostrup 2600

FINLAND
Ms. Anneli Wingfield
P.O. Box 1422
00101 Helsinki

FRANCE
Mr. Pierre de Proyart
7 Quai Voltaire
Paris 75007

Mr. Bernard Estournet
1 rue de l'Arrivée
Enghien-les-Bains 95880

GERMANY and AUSTRIA
Mr. Rudolf Walberg
P.O. Box 1544
D-65800 Bad Soden

Mr. Stephan Zipplies
Auf der Platt 20
61479 Glashuetten im Ts

SOS Study Centre - Frankfurt
In den Enterwiesen 4+9
D-61276, Weilrod-Riedelbach
Germany
☏ +49-6083-959-4700

GIBRALTAR
Mr. Sunder Mahtani
RSSB Charitable Trust -
Gibraltar
15 Rosia Road, GX11 1AA
☏ +350-200-412-67

GREECE
Mr. Themistoclis Gianopoulos
6 Platonos Str.
17672 Kallithea, Attiki

SOS Study Centre - Athens
10 Filikis Etaireias Street
14234-Nea Ionia, Attiki
☏ +30-210-7010610

ITALY
Mrs. Wilma Salvatori Torri
Via Bacchiglione 3
00199 Rome

Mr. Bill Kahn
Strada Statale 63, No. 189
42044 Santa Vittoria di
Gualtieri (RE)

NETHERLANDS
Mr. Henk Keuning
Kleizuwe2
3633 AE Vreeland

Science of the Soul Study
Centre - Netherlands
Middenweg 145 E
1394 AH Nederhorst den Berg
☏ +31-294-255-255

NORWAY
Mr. Manoj Kaushal
Langretta 8
N - 1279 Oslo

POLAND
Mr. Vinod Kumar Sharma
P.O. Box 59
Ul. Szkolna 15
05-090 Raszyn

PORTUGAL
Mrs. Sharda Lodhia
CRCA Portugal
Av. Coronel Eduardo Galhardo
No.18 A-B, Lisbon 1170-105

ROMANIA
Mrs. Carmen Cismas
C.P. 6-12, 810600 Braila

SLOVENIA
Mr. Marko Bedina
Brezje pri Trzicu 68
4290 Trzic

SPAIN
Mr. J. W. Balani
Fundacion Cultural RSSB -
Malaga
Avenida de las Americas s/n
Cruce Penon de Zapata
29130 Alhaurin de la Torre
Malaga
☏ +34-952-414-679

SWEDEN
Mr. Lennart Zachen
Norra Sonnarpsvägen 29
SE-286 72 Asljunga

SWITZERLAND
Mr. Sebastian Züst
Weissenrainstrasse 48
CH 8707 Uetikon Am See

UNITED KINGDOM
Mr. Narinder Singh Johal
SOS Study Centre - Haynes Park
Haynes Park, Church End
Haynes, MK45 3BL Bedford
☎ +44-1234-381-234

Mr. Douglas Cameron
SOS Study Centre - Haynes Park
Haynes Park, Church End
Haynes, MK45 3BL Bedford

AFRICA

BENIN
Mr. Jaikumar T. Vaswani
01 Boite Postale 951
Recette Principale, Cotonou 01

BOTSWANA
Dr. Krishan Lal Bhateja
P.O. Box 402539, Gaborone

CONGO-KINSHASA
Mr. Prahlad Parbhu
143 Kasai Ave., Lubumbashi

GHANA
Mr. Amrit Pal Singh
RSSB - Accra
P.O. Box 3976, Accra
☎ +233-242-057-309

IVORY COAST
Mr. Veerender Kumar Sapra
Avenue 7, Rue 19, Lot 196
Trechville
05 BP 1547 Abidjan 05

KENYA
Mr. Amarjit Singh Virdi
RSSB - Nairobi
P.O. Box 15134
Langata 00509, Nairobi
☎ +254-20-210-2970

LESOTHO
Mr. Tumelo Moseme
No.1 PTC Kofi Ammam Road
Maseru 0100

MADAGASCAR
Mrs. I. Rakotomahandry
BP100 Airport d'Ivato
Antananarivo 105

MAURITIUS
Mr. Indurlall Fagoonee
SOS - Mauritius
69 CNR Antelme /
Stanley Avenues
Quatre Bornes
☎ +230-454-3300

MOZAMBIQUE
Mr. Mangaram Matwani
Av Josina Machel
1st floor No. 376
Maputo 190

NAMIBIA
Mrs. Jennifer Carvill
P.O. Box 449
Swakopmund 9000

NIGERIA
Mr. Nanik N. Balani
G.P.O. Box 5054, Marina
Lagos

RÉUNION
Ms. Marie-Lynn Marcel
5 Chemin 'Gonneau, Bernica
St Gillesles Hauts 97435

SIERRA LEONE
Mr. Kishore S. Mahboobani
82/88 Kissy Dock Yard
P.O. Box 369, Freetown

SOUTH AFRICA
Mr. Gordon Clive Wilson
P.O. Box 1959
Randpark Ridge
Gauteng 2156

SOS Study Centre - Bush Hill
24 Kelly Road
Randburg, Bush Hill
Johannesburg 2092
☎ +27-11-025-7655

SWAZILAND
Mr. Mike Cox
Green Valley Farm
Malkerns

TANZANIA
Mr. Devender Singh Nagi
P.O. Box 1963
Dar es Salaam

UGANDA
Mr. Sylvester Kakooza
RSSB - Kampala
P.O. Box 31381, Kampala

ZAMBIA
Mr. Surinder Kumar Sachar
2922 Mutondo Crescent
Copper Belt, Kitwe 212

ZIMBABWE
Mr. Gordon Clive Wilson
P.O. Box 1959
Randpark Ridge
Gauteng 2156, South Africa

MIDDLE EAST

BAHRAIN
Mr. Sameer Deshpande
P.O. Box 75160
Juffair, Manama

ISRAEL
Mr. Michael Yaniv
Moshav Sde Nitzan 59
D.N. Hanegev 85470

KUWAIT
Mr. Jayakara Shetty
P.O. Box 22223
13083 Safat

U.A.E.
Mr. Daleep Dhalumal Jatwani
P.O. Box 37816, Dubai
☎ +971-4-339-4773